Mapping the Higher Education Landscape

HIGHER EDUCATION DYNAMICS

VOLUME 28

SCOPE OF THE SERIES

Higher Education Dynamics is a bookseries intending to study adaptation processes and their outcomes in higher education at all relevant levels. In addition it wants to examine the way interactions between these levels affect adaptation processes. It aims at applying general social science concepts and theories as well as testing theories in the field of higher education research. It wants to do so in a manner that is of relevance to all those professionally involved in higher education, be it as ministers, policy-makers, politicians, institutional leaders or administrators, higher education researchers, members of the academic staff of universities and colleges, or students. It will include both mature and developing systems of higher education, covering public as well as private institutions.

For other titles published in this series, go to
www.springer.com/series/6037

Frans A. van Vught
Editor

Mapping the Higher Education Landscape

Towards a European Classification
of Higher Education

 Springer

Editor
Frans A. van Vught
University of Twente
The Netherlands

ISBN 978-90-481-2248-6   e-ISBN 978-90-481-2249-3

Library of Congress Control Number: 2008936885

springer.com

Preface

This book is the result of a project focused on the development of an instrument able to create useful and effective transparency in the diversity of European higher education. The project has been undertaken by an international team of experts and has been sponsored by the European Commission. The book offers the conceptual, empirical and methodological frameworks relevant for the development of the transparency instrument. It founds this instrument in the theoretical and empirical literature about diversity in higher education systems. It places it in the contexts of the current supranational and national higher education policies in Europe. And it reports on the methodologies of design and research that have been applied.

Moreover, this book presents the first version of the instrument itself: the European classification of higher education institutions. In addition, it explores the potential use and applicability of such a classification, both at the levels of the European Higher Education and Research Areas (EHEA and ERA) and at the level of individual higher education institutions.

This book builds on two earlier reports. In August 2005 the report "Institutional Profiles" was published. This report is the result of the first phase of the project on the development of a European classification of higher education institutions. In general terms, the objectives of this first phase were:

- To assess the need for a European classification of higher education institutions
- To develop a conceptual model upon which such a classification could be based
- To propose an appropriate set of dimensions and indicators for such a classification

The first phase of the project resulted in a set of principles for designing a classification as well as a first draft of the components of such a classification (the draft classification). Both were produced in an elaborate process of consultation with identified stakeholders. A wide range of stakeholders showed interest in the project and contributed to a constructive and fruitful exchange of ideas and views regarding the classification.

At the end of the second phase of the project the report "Mapping Diversity" was produced (September 2008). The overall objectives of the second phase were:

- To test the draft classification developed in phase I and to adapt it to the realities and needs of the various stakeholders
- To explore and enhance the legitimacy of a European classification of higher education institutions

The second phase implied a set of empirical tests, resulting in an adapted second draft of the classification. In addition, a number of suggestions regarding its possible operational introduction were made.

This book contains the results of the first two phases of the project on building a European higher education classification. The classification presented in this book is a first version, which needs further analysis and fine-tuning. During the third and final phase of the project (which began in October 2008) a number of activities are undertaken that will eventually result in a firm proposal for a European classification of higher education institutions. The finalisation and implementation of this classification will be a major step in the further development of European higher education. It will create greater transparency and reveal the rich diversity of European higher education. In this sense it will map the European higher education landscape and help to create stronger profiles, of the system as a whole and of its many individual higher education institutions.

A process of stakeholder consultation and discussion has been the hallmark of this project since its inception in 2005. Many organisations have contributed to the development of the classification. We are thankful to all of them, but would especially like to mention the following organisations: Association Européenne des Conservatoires et des Académies de Musique (AEC), Association of Universities in the Netherlands (VSNU), Bologna Follow-Up Group (BFUG), Budapest Technical University, Coimbra Group, Compostela Group, Conference of Rectors of Academic Schools in Poland (CRASP), Conference of Rectors of Spanish Universities (CRUE), Council of Europe, European Association of Distance Teaching Universities (EADTU), European Association of Institutions in Higher Education (EURASHE), European Commission, European Consortium of Innovative Universities (ECIU), European Round Table of Industrialists (ERT), European Students' Union (ESU), European Trade Union Committee for Education (ETUCE), European University Association (EUA), Fachhochschule Osnabrück, Fachhochschule Vorarlberg, Fontys Hogescholen, Free University of Amsterdam, Hochschulrektorenkonferenz, Hungarian Rectors' Conference (MRK), International Association of Universities (IAU), International Research Universities Network (IRUN), League of European Research Universities (LERU), Norwegian Rectors' Conference (UHR), Norwegian University of Science and Technology, Organisation for Economic Development and Cooperation (OECD), Platform Aangewezen / Erkende Onderwijsinstellingen Nederland (PAEPON), Rectors' Conference of the Swiss Universities (CRUS), Rupert-Karls Universität Heidelberg, Royal College of Music (Sweden), UNESCO-CEPES, Universities of Applied Sciences (UAS), University of Calabria, University of Strathclyde, University of Twente, Universities UK.

Since the beginning of the project (in 2005) many persons have contributed to the design of the European classification of higher education institutions. Several of them have contributed to this book. The following individuals have been or still are member of the international project team: Jeroen Bartelse, David Bohmert, Nadine Burquel, Jindra Divis, Jon File, Christiane Gaehtgens, Saskia Hansen, Jeroen Huisman, Ben Jongbloed, Frans Kaiser, Rolf Peter, Sybille Reichert, Jim Taylor, Frans van Vught (project leader), Marijk van der Wende, Peter West, Don Westerheijden. Rose-Marie Barbeau and Ingrid van der Schoor have been invaluable in the production of this book.

As was indicated, the project has been funded with support from the European Commission, through the Lifelong Learning Programme (Socrates). This publication reflects the views of the authors and the Commission cannot be held responsible for any use which may be made of the information therein.

For more information on the European higher education classification, see: www.u-map.eu

Brussels, December 2008   Frans van Vught

Contents

Contributors

Dr. Jeroen Bartelse is director of the inter-ministerial Department of Knowledge and Innovation in the Netherlands and is affiliated as a researcher to the Centre for Higher Education Policy Studies (CHEPS). Dr Bartelse studied public administration at Erasmus University, Rotterdam and Indiana University, Indianapolis. In 1999, he obtained his Ph.D. in the field of higher education and research at CHEPS, University of Twente. He has participated in several international higher education advisory projects and held a position as policy advisor to the president of the University of Twente. From 2000 to 2006, he was head of policy of the Netherlands Association of Universities (VSNU). Dr Bartelse has held his current position since 2007. He has published on higher education and research throughout his career.

Professor Julie Feilberg has been Pro-Rector Education and Quality of Learning at the Norwegian University for Science and Technology (NTNU) since 2002. She served previously as associate professor in the Department of Applied Linguistics, Head of the Department of Applied Linguistics and Vice-Dean in the Faculty of Arts. Professor Feilberg has chaired and served on several national boards, committees and councils, and has for many years participated in large-scale research work dealing with the principal aspects of NTNU's activities. Her main area of research relates to organisational language development and communication.

Dr. Christiane Gaehtgens is an expert in higher education policy and its impact on the governance of research and higher education institutions at national, European and international levels. Dr Gaehtgens read German and Slavonic Studies and obtained a Ph.D. in Comparative Literature from the University of Bonn in 1987. In 1991 she was appointed Head of North America – Programmes of DAAD (German Academic Exchange Service). In 1994 she took a position as Director of the DAAD office in London/UK. In 1998 she became Secretary General of the then newly-founded Science Council of Lower Saxony in Hannover/ Germany. From 2003 to July 2008 she was Secretary General of the German Rectors' Conference (HRK), based in Bonn and Berlin. Dr Gaehtgens has recently established Impact-Consulting, a private consultancy advising universities and research institutions on issues of strategy, policy, internal governance and quality assurance.

Saskia Loer Hansen (MA) is currently the Head of Governance, Management and Policy at the University of Strathclyde. She was previously the University's Strategy Officer and closely involved in the development of Strathclyde's strategy "The Agenda for Excellence". From 2001 to 2008, Saskia served as Secretary to the European Consortium of Innovative Universities (ECIU) and supported the Consortium's activities including leadership development activities, new joint European masters programmes and liaison with the European Commission. Saskia is a graduate of Social Anthropology, Ethnography and European Studies from the University of Aarhus, Denmark, and worked at Aalborg University, Denmark, from 1998 to 2004.

Professor Jeroen Huisman is professor of Higher Education Management and director of the International Centre for Higher Education Management, University of Bath (UK). He is editor of *Higher Education Policy* and co-editor of *Tertiary Education and Management*. His current research interests include higher education governance; leadership and management; institutional diversity; internationalisation and globalisation; and Europeanisation and the Bologna process. Two recent book publications are: Kehm, Huisman & Stensaker (eds. 2008), *The European Higher Education Area: Perspectives on a Moving Target* (Sense Publishers) and Huisman (ed. 2009) *International Perspectives on the Governance of Higher Education: Alternative Frameworks for Coordination* (Routledge).

Frans Kaiser (MA) is senior research associate at the Center for Higher Education Policy Studies (CHEPS). His background is in public administration. He has over a decade's experience in large comparative studies in higher education, both from a qualitative and a quantitative perspective. Mr Kaiser is an expert in international comparison of higher education systems and policies, as well as in the design and use of indicators for international comparison and has conducted several international studies and projects and published on comparative issues, indicators, funding and governance in higher education.

Professor Astrid Laegreid is professor of functional genomics specialising in molecular biology and Pro-Rector Research and Innovation at the Norwegian University of Science and Technology (NTNU) in Trondheim. She has initiated and led several large, multidisciplinary projects that use a systems biology approach to cancer research. She gained managerial experience as Vice Dean of the Faculty of Medicine, and has served on university and governmental committees addressing medical technology, functional genomics, research ethics, equal gender opportunities, academic leadership training and young researcher recruitment.

Dr Rolf Peter holds a Ph.D. degree in Social Sciences from the University of Mannheim, Germany. His career includes intensive research in International Relations and European Integration Studies at the Mannheim Centre for European Social Research and the Center for European Integration Studies, Bonn. Working in the International Department of the German Rectors' Conference (HRK) since 2005, he is currently in charge of the section "Academic Reforms in Europe". He has also been coordinator of and expert consultant to several international consulting projects on behalf of HRK, which mainly focused on institutional development in higher education systems in the Balkans and Eastern Europe.

Dr. Sybille Reichert holds a Ph.D. from Yale University (1994). She has been head of strategic planning at the ETH Zürich. Since 2004 she has headed her own consultancy firm, specialising in policy and strategy studies and development projects in higher education for European organisations, national ministries, rectors' conferences and individual universities. She has undertaken several large studies, including the European University Association's Trends III and IV reports (2003, 2005) which looked at the implications of the Bologna reforms for institutional development in Europe. In addition Dr Reichert has conducted strategy coaching projects for several universities and participates frequently in university evaluations at faculty, institutional, network or system level.

Professor Dirk Van Damme is Head of CERI (Centre for Educational Research and Innovation) at OECD in Paris. He holds a Ph.D. degree in educational sciences from Ghent University and has also been also professor of educational sciences at that university (since 1995), as well as part-time professor in comparative education at the Free University of Brussels (1997–2000) and visiting professor of comparative education at Seton Hall University, NJ, USA (2001–2008). Professor van Damme has been professionally involved in educational policy development as deputy director of the cabinet of Flemish Minister of Education Luc van den Bossche (1992–1998), general director of the Flemish rectors' conference VLIR (2000–2003), expert consultant on the implementation of the Bologna Declaration for Flemish Minister of Education Marleen Vanderpoorten (2002–2003) and director of the cabinet for Flemish Minister of Education Frank Vandenbroucke (2004–2008). Prof van Damme has served as an expert advisor on international higher education policy, quality assurance and accreditation issues for several international organisations.

Professor Marijk Van Der Wende is professor of higher education at the Free University of Amsterdam and a visiting professor at the Centre for Higher Education Policy Studies (CHEPS) at the University of Twente. Her research focuses on innovation in higher education, the impact of globalisation on higher education and related processes of internationalisation and Europeanisation. She published widely on how these processes affect higher education systems, their structure and governance, institutional strategies, curriculum design, quality assurance methods, and the use of technology. Marijk is the President of the Governing Board of the Programme on Institutional Management in Higher Education (IMHE) of the OECD (2005–2009). She is the founding dean of Amsterdam University College, an international liberal arts & science college established jointly by the Free University of Amsterdam and the University of Amsterdam.

Professor Frans Van Vught leads the project on the European higher education classification. He was the founding director (1984–1996) of the Center for Higher Education Policy Studies (CHEPS) and President and Rector of the University of Twente (1997–2005). He is currently President of the European Center for Strategic Management of Universities (ESMU), Chairman of the Board of the Netherlands'

House for Education and Research (Nether) and policy advisor to the President of the European Commission. He is a member of national higher education councils in various countries in the world and has been a consultant to many international organisations, national governments and higher education institutions. Professor Van Vught is a sought-after speaker, holds several honorary doctorates, and has published widely on higher education. Recent book publication: Dill & Van Vught (eds. 2009), *National Innovation and the Academic Research Enterprise, Public Policy in International Perspective* (Johns Hopkins University Press, Baltimore, MD).

Dr. Peter West is Secretary to the University of Strathclyde, responsible for all the professional services of the University. He is a graduate in Modern History from the University of St Andrews. He was president of the OECD's Institutional Management for Higher Education (IMHE) programme from 1998 to 2002 and currently chairs the Scotland/Malawi Partnership, which is building a unique relationship between the two countries. He is a regular speaker at international conferences on higher education management and several of his papers have been published. Dr West has been awarded honorary doctorates by the Universities of Rostov-on-Don, Russia (1996) and Malawi (2002). He was awarded the OBE for services to Higher Education in Scotland and Malawi in 2006.

Dr. Don Westerheijden works as senior research associate at the Centre for Higher Education Policy Studies (CHEPS) of the University of Twente, where he coordinates research related to quality management and is involved in the coordination of Ph.D. students. He is a member of the editorial boards of several journals related to quality in higher education. His research interests include institutional and systematic impacts of internal and external evaluation of quality (of education, research, and of institutions) in Europe, impacts of the Bologna process and impacts of rankings. Among other affiliations, Dr Westerheijden is a member of the expert panel of Studychoice123.nl and the scientific steering group of the Austrian accreditation agency AQA.

Chapter 1
Diversity and Differentiation in Higher Education[1]

Frans van Vught

1.1 Introduction

This chapter addresses the concepts of diversity and differentiation in higher education. It explores the literature regarding these concepts and offers a conceptual framework which seeks to explain why processes of differentiation and dedifferentiation take place in higher education systems.

When discussing external diversity and processes of system differentiation, we will discuss the behaviour of the various "actors" in the system. These actors to a large extent are the higher education organisations that are part of a higher education system. We will interpret these organisations as "corporate actors" (Coleman 1990, p. 531), and will assume that the explanation of social phenomena like differentiation and diversity is possible by means of analysing the behaviour and/or opinions of these corporate actors who need not necessarily be natural persons (although the activities of corporate actors are of course carried out by people).

In the higher education literature several forms of diversity are mentioned. In a survey of the literature Birnbaum (1983) identifies seven categories that are largely related to external diversity (Huisman 1995):

- *Systemic diversity* refers to differences in institutional type, size and control found within a higher education system.
- *Structural diversity* refers to institutional differences resulting from historical and legal foundations, or differences in the internal division of authority among institutions.
- *Programmatic diversity* relates to the degree level, degree area, comprehensiveness, mission and emphasis of programmes and services provided by institutions.
- *Procedural diversity* describes differences in the ways in which teaching, research and/or services are provided by institutions.

---

[1]This chapter is a shortened and adapted version of: Frans van Vught, Mission Diversity and Reputation in Higher Education, in: *Higher Education Policy*, 2008, 21(2) 151–174, International Association of Universities, reproduced with the permission of Palgrave Macmillan Publishers, Ltd.

- *Reputational diversity* communicates the perceived differences in institutions based on status and prestige.
- *Constituential diversity* alludes to differences in students served and other constituents in the institutions (faculty, administration).
- *Value and climate diversity* is associated with differences in social environment and culture.

For our purposes, the distinction between external and internal diversity is the crucial one. We will focus on the differences *between* institutions rather than on differences *within* institutions, but we will take differences in their programmes (of teaching and research) into account. In this book we will use the term *institutional diversity* to describe the external diversity in higher education systems. An important distinction regarding institutional diversity, which we will also use in this volume, is the one between vertical and horizontal diversity (Teichler 2007a, b). Vertical diversity is understood to address differences between higher education institutions in terms of (academic) prestige and reputation. Horizontal diversity regards differences in institutional missions and profiles.

1.2   Classical Studies

Generally speaking, the first comprehensive study on diversity and differentiation is Charles Darwin's *Origin of Species* published in 1859. Darwin's explanation of evolution and biological diversity was definitely radical for the time. He argued that diversity results not from divine creation or an overall master plan, but from an undirected, random process of adaptation to environmental circumstances in combination with successful sexual reproduction. Darwin's original theory of natural selection has been refined and supplemented over the years, but his basic concepts are still judged to be valid and have inspired many other theoretical frameworks.

Differentiation also has become a well-known concept in the social sciences. Here the first study of differentiation is of course Durkheim's classic *The Division of Labor in Society* (1893). Building on Durkheim (and Weber), Parsons designed his famous structural-functionalist conceptualisation of differentiation (Parsons 1966).

Since Durkheim, many social scientists have contributed to the further theoretical conceptualisation of differentiation processes. However, as Rhoades (1990) points out, these contributions are directed to the effects rather than the causes of differentiation. In the evolutionary approach to differentiation, which has its roots in the classical studies of Marx and Spencer, differentiation is seen mainly as an element in the "adaptive processes of social systems which retain these structures, processes, etc. that lead to greater adaptation to the environment" (Campbell 1965, p. 16). Similarly, the functionalists focus on the assumed needs and functions of social systems and hence tend to see differentiation as a component in a process of enhancing the adaptive capacity and the efficiency of social systems (Merton 1968).

Nevertheless, the social sciences appear to contain less of an explanatory mechanism for processes of differentiation leading to higher levels of diversity than the biological theory of natural selection. The most powerful social science explanation of differentiation actually comes very close to the biological explanation. Particularly based on economic theory, it often is argued that market mechanisms result in processes of differentiation and create optimum levels of diversity in a system. In analogy to the biological theory of natural selection, competition among social actors is assumed to select the strongest or the best in a certain context, while stimulating all actors to find niches to which they are best suited. The crucial difference between biological natural selection and market-driven adaptation is of course that social actors' behaviour is purposive and non-random. In social contexts rationality is part of the game. The next section introduces some of the more recent perspectives in organisational sociology that specifically address this issue of purposive behaviour in social systems.

1.3   Recent Perspectives

The explanatory framework to be presented later in this chapter draws heavily on three theoretical perspectives from organisational theory: the population ecology perspective, the resource dependency perspective and the institutional isomorphism perspective. Although these three perspectives have much in common, there are also some specific differences.

The population ecology approach is based on the Darwinian evolutionary point of view. According to Hannan and Freeman, two of the most important authors in this field, the population ecology approach concentrates "on the sources of variability and homogeneity of organisational forms.... In doing so, it pays considerable attention to population dynamics, especially the processes of competition among diverse organisations for limited resources such as membership, capital and legitimacy" (1989, p. 13).

The resource dependency perspective stresses the mutual processes of interaction between organisations and their environments. According to this approach, organisations on the one hand are dependent on their environments (which primarily consist of other organisations) but on the other hand these organisations are also able to influence their environments. "Rather than taking the environment as a given to which the organisation then adapts, it is considerably more realistic to consider the environment as an outcome of a process that involves both adaptation to the environment and attempts to change that environment" (Pfeffer & Salancik 1978, p. 222).

The institutional isomorphism approach stresses that in order to survive, organisations have to adapt to the existence of and pressures by other organisations in their environment. These adaptation processes tend to lead to homogenisation, as organisations react more or less similarly to uniform environmental conditions. Isomorphism is a constraining process that forces organisations to resemble other organisations that face the same set of environmental conditions (DiMaggio & Powell 1983).

Further on, the theoretical notions of these three perspectives are used to develop a conceptual framework that intends to explain the processes of differentiation and dedifferentiation in higher education systems. Before doing so, let us first focus on the various arguments in favour of diversity and differentiation in higher education systems, and let us address the most relevant studies on these concepts in the literature.

1.4 Arguments in Favour of Diversity

Diversity has been identified in the higher education literature as one of the major factors associated with the positive performance of higher education systems. Birnbaum (1983) presents an overview of the various arguments found in the literature in favour of institutional diversity (which I have adapted somewhat). Many of these arguments appear to be highly relevant in the context of higher education policy-making.

First, it is often argued that increased diversity in a higher education system is an important strategy to meet student needs. A more diversified system is assumed to be better able to offer access to higher education to students with different educational backgrounds and with varied histories of academic achievements. The argument is that in a diversified system, in which the performance of higher education institutions varies, each student is offered an opportunity to work and compete with students of similar background. Each student has the opportunity to find an educational environment in which chances for success are realistic.

A second and related argument is that diversity provides for social mobility. By offering different modes of entry into higher education and by providing multiple forms of transfer, a diversified system stimulates upward mobility as well as honourable downward mobility. A diversified system allows for corrections of errors of choice; it provides extra opportunities for success; it rectifies poor motivation; and it broadens educational horizons.

Third, diversity is supposed to meet the needs of the labour market. The point of view here is that in modern society an increasing variety of specialisations on the labour market is necessary to allow further economic and social development. A homogeneous higher education system is thought to be less able to respond to the diverse needs of the labour market than a diversified system.

A fourth argument is that diversity serves the political needs of interest groups. The idea is that a diverse system ensures the needs of different groups in society to have their own identity and their own political legitimacy. In less diversified higher education systems the needs of specific groups may remain unaddressed, which may cause internal debates in a higher education system.

A fifth and well-known argument is that diversity permits the crucial combination of élite and mass higher education. Generally speaking, mass systems tend to be more diversified than élite systems, as mass systems absorb a more heterogeneous clientele and attempt to respond to a wider range of demands from the labour market. In his famous analysis of mass and élite systems, Trow (1979) has indicated that the survival of élite higher education depends on the existence of a comprehensive system of non-élite institutions. Essentially, Trow argues that only if a majority of the students are offered the knowledge and skills that are relevant to find a position in the labour market will a few élite institutions be able to survive.

A sixth reason why diversity is an important objective for higher education systems is that diversity is assumed to increase the level of effectiveness of higher education institutions. This argument is made for instance by the Carnegie Commission (1973) which has suggested that institutional specialisation allows higher education institutions to focus their attention and energy, and thus achieve higher levels of effectiveness.

Finally, diversity is assumed to offer opportunities for experimenting with innovation. In diversified higher education systems, institutions have the option to assess the viability of innovations created by other institutions, without necessarily having to implement these innovations themselves. Diversity offers the possibility to explore the effects of innovative behaviour without the need to implement the innovation for all institutions at the same time. Diversity permits low-risk experimentation.

These various arguments in favour of institutional diversity show that diversity is usually assumed to be a worthwhile objective for higher education systems. Diversified higher education systems are supposed to produce higher levels of client-orientation (both regarding the needs of students and of the labour market), social mobility, effectiveness, flexibility, innovativeness and stability. More diversified systems, generally speaking, are thought to be "better" than less diversified systems. And many governments have designed and implemented policies to increase the level of diversity of higher education systems.

Unfortunately, it is not always clear how an increase in a higher education system's diversity should be realised. The many governmental policies that have been developed and implemented do not always lead to the desired results. It appears that, although these concepts have a long tradition in the social sciences, diversity and differentiation are still only partly understood.

1.5 Studies on Differentiation and Diversity in Higher Education

The concepts of diversity and differentiation have been widely discussed in the higher education literature. In this section, a brief categorisation of the most influential studies is presented (for a more elaborate overview, see Huisman 1995).

It appears that many studies on diversity and differentiation in higher education can be distinguished according to the question of whether differentiation or dedifferentiation processes are assumed to take place in higher education systems.

On the one hand there are studies that claim that higher education systems show an immanent drive towards differentiation and increasing levels of diversity. On the other hand there are studies that argue that higher education systems are characterised by dedifferentiation and decreasing levels of diversity.

Examples of the category of studies claiming an immanent drive towards increasing levels of diversity are Parsons and Platt (1973) and Clark (1978). In their well-known study on the US higher education system, Parsons and Platt discuss, in addition to several other themes, the processes of differentiation within higher education systems. Their main argument appears to be that processes of differentiation occur when new functions emerge in a system. An example is the development of graduate schools, which have come to be differentiated from undergraduate colleges. However, differentiation apparently does not necessarily imply the coming into existence of a new type of organisation, as the authors also argue that new functions can be integrated in existing organisations.

Clark's argument regarding diversity and differentiation is based on his conviction that the growing complexity of bodies of knowledge brings along an ever-increasing fragmentation within and among higher education organisations. According to Clark (1983), the increasing complexity of higher education systems (and of the functions this system must fulfil) is an outcome of three related forces: the increasing variety of the student population, the growth of the labour market for academic graduates and the emergence and growth of new disciplines. The effects are ongoing differentiation processes and increasing levels of diversity. Emphasising that differentiation often is in the interest of groups and individuals, Clark underlines the immanent drive towards differentiation in higher education: "Once created and made valuable to a group, often to an alliance of groups, academic forms persist. Out of successive historical periods come additional forms, with birth rate greatly exceeding death rate. Differentiation is then an accumulation of historical deposits" (Clark 1983, p. 221).

Next to the studies that claim that higher education systems show a more or less permanent drive towards differentiation stand the studies that argue that *de*differentiation is the name of the higher education game. Examples of this category of studies are Riesman (1956), Birnbaum (1983), and Rhoades (1990). In his classical study *Constraint and Variety in American Education* (1956), Riesman compares the US higher education system with a kind of reptilian procession during which certain higher education institutions will move to the positions where other institutions were before. According to Riesman, this procession is the result of the typical behaviour of higher education institutions, which basically consists of lower status institutions trying to gain status by imitating higher status institutions (especially the prestigious research universities). This imitating behaviour, also indicated as "academic drift" (Neave 1979), creates a tendency towards uniformity and decreasing levels of diversity.

Birnbaum (1983) not only presents an elaborate classification on forms of diversity (in which seven forms of diversity are identified), he also tries to empirically assess the changes in external diversity in the US higher education system between 1960 and 1980. His findings show that during this period the number of institutional types had not increased and thus that differentiation had not occurred. Birnbaum hypothesises that especially centralised state-level planning and the application of rigid criteria for the approval of new institutions and programmes hamper differentiation processes. Governmental policies, says Birnbaum, may be a major factor in producing processes of dedifferentiation and decreasing levels of diversity.

Rhoades' (1990) argument is that processes of dedifferentiation are the result of political competition between academic professionals and (external) lay groups, and governmental policies that structure these processes of competition. Rhoades indicates that as an effect of governmental policies and administrative systems in higher education, the power of the academic professionals is often quite large. The power balance between academics and lay groups to a large extent determines whether differentiation actually occurs. Comparing the developments in the higher education systems of the UK, France, Sweden and the US, Rhoades concludes that academics have been successful in defending their own norms and values and hence have prevented differentiation processes from taking place.

The various studies just presented show that institutional diversity and differentiation have been regularly addressed by higher education scholars. However, these studies also show that rather different points of view appear to exist regarding the direction of differentiation or dedifferentiation processes in higher education systems. Are these systems showing an immanent drive towards differentiation because of the emergence of new functions (Parsons & Platt) or because of the growing complexities of the bodies of knowledge and the variety of the student body and the labour market (Clark)? Or are systems of higher education to be characterised by immanent processes of dedifferentiation because of the imitating behaviour of lower status institutions (Riesman), centralised and uniform governmental policies (Birnbaum), or academic conservatism (Rhoades)?

In the following section some of these factors are combined into a conceptual framework which seeks to explain institutional diversity in higher education systems.

1.6 A Theoretical Framework for Explaining Differentiation and Diversity in Higher Education Systems

In this paragraph, the framework for a theory of differentiation and diversity in higher education systems will be sketched. Our point of departure will be the well-known "open systems" approach in the social sciences. Using this approach, we interpret higher education as a system consisting of individual higher education organisations (being the components – or subsystems – of the higher education system) embedded in an environment which includes the social, political and economic conditions within which the higher education organisations need to operate. Being an open system, the higher education system is open to its environment, which implies that its components are both able to receive inputs (in the form of students, faculty, finances, and other resources) and to deliver outputs (in the form of graduates, research, results and advice). This leads us to a first assumption for the theoretical framework:

Assumption 1: **Organisations for higher education receive inputs from and produce outputs for their environments.**
To the still rather general open systems approach, we add the three (mutually related) theoretical perspectives from organisational theory that were briefly introduced earlier: the population ecology perspective, the resource dependency perspective and the institutional isomorphism perspective.

The population ecology perspective has been sketched by Morgan (1986, p. 66) in the following terms: "Organisations, like organisms in nature, depend for survival on their ability to acquire an adequate supply of resources necessary to sustain existence. In this effort they have to face competition with other organisations, and since there is usually a resource scarcity, only the fittest survive. The nature, number and distribution of organisations at any given time is dependent on resource availability and on competition within and between different species of organisations."

In the population ecology model, the environment is the critical factor. The environment determines which organisations succeed and which fail. The environment acts as the critical selector. This point of view is clearly based on the Darwinian evolutionary perspective of variation, selection and retention. Variation may take place by means of various sources (planning, but also error, chance, luck and conflict; see Aldrich 1979, p. 28). Selection is the process by which the organisations that fit particular environmental conditions are positively selected. Retention is the process in which the selected variations are preserved (Aldrich 1979, pp. 28–31).

There are a few theoretical notions of the population ecology perspective that need our special attention. One is that the theoretical model is directed to understanding the dynamics of whole populations of organisations rather than of individual organisations. In the work by Aldrich, Hannan and Freeman, and others, the population ecology perspective refers to the aggregate study of organisations, that is, the organisations that fall within a certain "population". The emphasis of the theoretical model is on the rise and decline of different species of organisations, as well as on their shared characteristics.

This focus on populations of organisations is less relevant for our purposes. Given the wish to develop a theoretical framework for the explanation of differentiation and diversity in higher education systems, a focus on the rise and decline of species of organisations (and hence on a very large timeframe) appears to be less fruitful. Rather, the theoretical framework should address the ways by which processes of differentiation take place in higher education systems, as well as the resulting levels of diversity.

Another crucial insight of the population ecology model (as already indicated) is the idea that it is the ability of organisations to acquire relevant environmental resources (i.e., to obtain a resource niche) that is most important for success and survival. Organisations need an input of resources from their environment to be able to sustain existence. When resources are scarce, those organisations that are better able to secure a more or less permanent input have a better chance of survival.

Related to this notion is the important emphasis on competition. In the population ecologists' view, the process of competition for scarce resources will show which organisations are able to outperform their competitors and hence have a better chance to find a successful resource niche.

From the population ecology perspective we take two further assumptions for a theory of differentiation and diversity in higher education systems:

Assumption 2: **In order to survive, higher education organisations need to secure a continuous and sufficient supply of resources from their environments.**

Assumption 3: **When scarcity of resources exists, higher education organisations compete with each other to secure a continuous and sufficient supply of resources.**

This brings us to the important concept of structural isomorphism. In the population ecology perspective the competition between organisations produces a certain correspondence between, on the one hand, the environmental conditions (resources and constraints) and, on the other hand, the structural characteristics of organisations. According to Hannan and Freeman, the diversity of organisational forms is proportional to the diversity of resources and constraints in their environments (Hannan & Freeman 1989, p. 62). These authors also claim that the competition for scarce resources causes competing organisations to become similar. The conditions of competition lead to similar organisational responses and, moreover, to the elimination of the (dissimilar) weaker organisations. The result is an increase of homogeneity (structural isomorphism) (Hannan & Freeman 1977, p. 939).

However, the population ecology perspective has been criticised for exactly this notion of decreasing diversity under conditions of competition for scarce resources. Hawley (1986), for instance, contests Hannan and Freeman's assumption that competition for scarce resources causes structural isomorphism: "As a type of relation, competition is readily observable; as a producer of particular outcomes it is obscure. At most it helps account for the elimination of some contestants from a share of the limited resource" (Hawley 1986, p. 127). Apparently the relationships between environmental conditions, competition and diversity need further exploration.

At this point we turn to the two other (and related) perspectives from organisational theory: the resource dependency perspective and the institutional isomorphism perspective.

Although closely related to the population ecology perspective, the resource dependency perspective also shows an important distinction. While the population ecology model tends to emphasise the unidirectional organisational dependency on environmental conditions, the resource dependency model underlines the idea of mutual influencing. The environment certainly is perceived as having a major impact on organisational behaviour but, at the same time, organisations are also assumed to have certain effects on their environment. Pfeffer and Salancik (1978, p. 222) state this point of view as follows: "The view that organisations are constrained by their political, legal and social environment is only partially correct … organisations are not only constrained by their environments but … in fact, law, legitimacy and political outcomes somewhat reflect the actions taken by organisations to modify their environments for their interests in survival, growth and certainty."

We follow this line of argument and I assume that organisations (also in higher education) are affected by their environmental conditions, but are also able to affect these conditions.

Assumption 4: **Higher education organisations both influence and are influenced by their environmental conditions.**
Returning to the relationships between environmental conditions, competition and diversity, we are now not only able to formulate the expectation that competition for scarce resources forces organisations to more or less similar responses, but also that, when confronted with scarcity of resources, organisations may want to try to influence their environmental conditions in order to secure better conditions. To the notion of the population ecology perspective of structural isomorphism as a result of competition for scarce resources, we now add the insight from the resource dependency perspective that, confronted with scarcity, organisations can act to influence their environment. The remaining question of course is *how* organisations tend to act when their supply of resources is threatened. To find an answer to this question, let us look at the perspective of institutional isomorphism.

The basic view of this perspective is that the survival and success of organisations depend upon taking account of other organisations in the environment. According to DiMaggio and Powell (1983), this leads to three forms of institutional isomorphism, all leading to an increasing similarity in organisational behaviour and producing a decrease of systems diversity. Coercive isomorphism results from the pressures applied by other organisations (in the environment) on which the organisation is dependent (e.g., governmental policies and laws). Mimetic isomorphism stems from uncertainty caused by poorly understood technologies, ambiguous goals and the symbolic environment, which induces organisations to imitate the behaviour of perceived successful organisations. Normative isomorphism stems from professionalisation. Professionalism leads to homogeneity both because formal professional training produces a certain similarity in professional background and because membership of professional networks further encourages such a similarity.

It may be clear from these three forms of institutional isomorphism that, according to DiMaggio and Powell, both certain environmental conditions (e.g., governmental policies) and specific organisational characteristics (e.g., the perceived uncertainty of the environment and the degree of professionalisation of the organisation) may produce dedifferentiation processes. The argument appears to be that, confronted with scarcity of resources, organisations may either be forced to react in such a way that dedifferentiation processes occur, or they may themselves show a behaviour that contributes to a decrease in the external diversity of the overall system.

Using the insights from the three perspectives of organisational theory we may now formulate some general relationships between, on the one hand, environmental conditions and (de)differentiation, and, on the other hand, organisational behaviour and (de)differentiation. Keeping in mind the factors suggested in the higher education literature, a first proposition could be that the level of uniformity/variety of the environment of the organisation is related (by means of the organisation's adaptive behaviour) to the level of diversity of the higher education system. This proposition follows the notion of the population ecology model of competition under conditions of scarce resources; it underscores the argument of coercive isomorphism and accepts the idea that it is the organisation itself that shows the relevant adaptive behaviour.

Proposition 1: **The larger the uniformity of the environmental conditions of higher education organisations, the lower the level of diversity of the higher education system.**
Relevant factors from the higher education literature that could be used to test this proposition are: the level of uniformity of governmental policies (Birnbaum) and the level of variety in the student body and in the needs of the labour market (Clark).

A second proposition can be formulated when we focus on the general relationship between organisational behaviour and (de)differentiation. Again referring to some of the factors mentioned in the higher education literature (see above), the proposition could be that the level of influence of academic norms and values in a higher education organisation is related (by means of either academic professionalism or imitating behaviour) to the level of diversity of the higher education system. Also this proposition follows the notion of competition under conditions of scarce resources; it emphasises the arguments of mimetic and normative isomorphism and accepts the ability of the organisation to choose its own behaviour.

Proposition 2: **The larger the influence of academic norms and values in a higher education organisation, the lower the level of diversity of the higher education system.**
Relevant factors from the higher education literature to test this proposition are: the ability of academic professionals to define and defend the (academic) norms and values as relevant for higher education organisations (Rhoades) and the extent to which academic norms and values guide the imitating behaviour by lower status institutions (academic drift) (Riesman).

The two propositions offer a combination of structural isomorphism caused by competition (from the population ecology model) and institutional isomorphism caused by coercive, mimetic and normative pressures (from the institutional isomorphism model). In addition, the propositions show that the actual occurrence of processes of differentiation and dedifferentiation has to be explained by the combination of (external) environmental conditions and (internal) organisational characteristics. Either the tension between or the joining of these forces can offer a coherent explanation for processes of differentiation or dedifferentiation and thus for lower or higher levels of institutional diversity in a higher education system.

1.7 Higher Education Research Outcomes

Let us now return to the higher education literature and try to find some empirical indications that may be related to the conceptual framework. Are there outcomes of empirical higher education research that are relevant for testing our theoretical notions?

There appear to be remarkably few studies that produce empirical outcomes on diversity and differentiation in higher education. A few relevant studies can be mentioned. Huisman, Meek and Wood (2007) recently undertook a cross-national and longitudinal analysis of ten higher education systems. They found that, generally speaking, system size (the number of higher education institutions in a system) does not necessarily imply a high level of diversity. In addition, it appeared that governmental regulation may help to preserve a formally existing level of diversity in a higher education system, but that government-initiated merger operations bring about more homogeneity rather than an increase of diversity. The explanation offered by the authors is in line with our conceptual framework. They suggest that legally mandated boundaries in higher education systems (as for instance in legally regulated binary systems) are preserving the existing level of diversity, but that governmental policies that offer more autonomy to higher education institutions encourage these institutions to emulate the most prestigious ones.

The already mentioned studies by both Birnbaum (1983) and Rhoades (1990) also appear to offer empirical support for the theoretical framework presented. Birnbaum found that during the period 1960–1980 the institutional diversity of the US higher education system had not increased although the system had grown enormously. "It appears that the higher education system has used the vast increase in resources primarily to replicate existing forms (such as the community college) rather than to create new ones" (Birnbaum 1983, p. 144). In a recent study Morphew has repeated Birnbaum's study for the period 1972–2002. His findings reveal that, although the study period exhibited great change in the US higher education system, there is zero (or negative) growth in the general diversity of US higher education (Morphew 2006).

Rhoades (1990) compared the developments in the higher education systems of the UK, France, Sweden and the US between 1960 and 1980. His general finding appears to be that, although these systems show a certain amount of change, the processes of dedifferentiation were predominant. Rhoades expected that, because of a decrease in the financial resources for higher education during this period, the competition between the higher education institutions would increase, which would produce an increase in diversity. While discussing his empirical findings, he on the one hand suggests that several of the governments of the four countries have taken initiatives to introduce new types of institutions, but he also concludes that these governments (as well as accreditation boards) have contributed to dedifferentiation. In addition, Rhoades argues, it appears that in the four countries the influence of academic professionals in particular has been substantial. Academics appear to be able to define and monopolise the nature of their professional activities, and, by doing so, preserve the existing *status quo*. Academic professionals appear to be successful in resisting initiatives to change the system and in inhibiting processes of differentiation.

Several other empirical studies on differentiation in higher education systems appear to point in the same direction. In an analysis of differentiation processes in the Canadian higher education system, Skolnik (1986) comes to conclusions that are rather similar to the ones formulated by Birnbaum and Rhoades. According to Skolnik, the Canadian higher education system is faced with pressures towards homogenisation because of both the restricting provincial steering approaches and the strong dominance of the values and norms of academic professionals.

In a study of the changes in the Dutch higher education system, Maassen and Potman (1990) analysed the university "development plans". Their objective was to find out whether the universities had been able to use their enlarged autonomy (the result of new governmental policy) to create more diversity in the system. Their conclusion is negative: "… innovations all seem to go into the same direction of homogenisation. As far as the development plans are concerned, the institutions have not succeeded in establishing meaningful and discriminating profiles. On the contrary, it seems likely that various homogenising developments will emerge" (Maassen & Potman 1990, p. 403). According to the authors, the combination of governmental regulations and the power of the academic professionals (especially in the quality control system) explains the trend towards decreasing diversity.

Meek (1991) has analysed the structural changes in the Australian higher education system. An increase of institutional autonomy, the demise of the binary system and a large-scale merger operation were assumed to allow for more diversity in the system. According to Meek, the strong academic values and norms as well as the processes of academic drift tend to inhibit the increase of diversity. Dedifferentiation rather than differentiation appears to be the case in the Australian system.

The various empirical studies appear to underline the notions of the theoretical framework presented earlier. According to the authors of these studies, environmental pressures (especially governmental regulation) as well as the dominance of academic norms and values are the crucial factors that influence the processes of differentiation and dedifferentiation in higher education systems. In all cases, the empirical observations point in the direction of dedifferentiation and decreasing levels of diversity. The overall impression is that, in empirical reality, the combination of strict and uniform governmental policies and the predominance of academic norms and values leads to homogenisation.

However, it should be kept in mind that the theoretical framework also suggests other possible outcomes. When the environmental conditions are varied and when the influence of academic norms and values in a higher education institution is limited, the level of systems diversity may be expected to increase. Also, according to the theoretical framework, the combinations of uniform environmental conditions and limited influence of academic norms and values on the one hand, and of varied environmental conditions and large influence of academic norms and values on the other, might be related to either increasing or decreasing levels of diversity.

In addition, it may be pointed out that the pressures from governmental regulation do not necessarily have to be seen as mechanisms for homogenisation. As has been indicated by Huisman et al. and Rhoades, governmental policies may also play an important role in maintaining existing and formally regulated levels of diversity, if necessary, by containing academic conservatism and/or imitating behaviour by lower status institutions. From this point of view, the regulatory policy regarding the complex tripartite structure of the public sector higher education system of

California appears to be interesting. Although tensions exist within this system, it appears that the California Master Plan has succeeded in preventing homogenisation processes from occurring. A conscious legislative decision to maintain a certain level of diversity in the public system apparently has been able to restrain academic drift (Fox 1993).

A recent and interesting approach to maintaining and even increasing the diversity of a higher education system is the process followed by the University Grants Committee (UGC) of Hong Kong. The UGC entered into an open discussion with each of the (eight) universities of the Hong Kong higher education system and stimulated them to formulate their specific missions and roles in the context of the broader system. Subsequently, these missions and roles were formalised in agreements between the individual institutions and the UGC. During this process the UGC kept an eye on its objective to increase the diversity at the level of the system. Finally, after a few years, the UGC developed a Performance and Role-related Funding Scheme in which it explored, together with the individual institutions, whether they had been able to remain within the parameters of their mission and role statements. The result was a clear increase of the diversity of the Hong Kong higher education system and even a growing enthusiasm within the institutions to stick to their roles.

1.8   Conclusion

In this chapter we have discussed both the theoretical and empirical literature on diversity and differentiation in higher education. We explored some relevant theoretical perspectives in especially organisational theory that intend to explain processes of differentiation and dedifferentiation in social systems. We constructed our own conceptual framework seeking to explain why processes of (de)differentiation take place in systems of higher education, and we confronted this framework with the relevant outcomes of empirical higher education research.

Our conclusion is that two sets of variables appear to be crucial in the processes of differentiation and dedifferentiation in higher education systems. One set of variables regards the environmental conditions with which higher education institutions are being confronted and that to a large extent influence the behaviour of these organisations. In this set of variables in particular governmental regulation and policies appear to be highly influential factors. At the same time, it appears that market forces do not necessarily lead to increasing diversity. The second category of variables relates to the impact of professionalism in higher education, particularly as a normative mechanism influencing the dynamics of professional behaviour. The dominance of certain (academic) norms and values (through professional training and networks) has a major impact on (de)differentiation processes in higher education systems.

We also noted that uniformity of environmental conditions and of academic norms and values appear to lead to homogenisation in higher education systems.

Higher levels of diversity of contextual conditions and of normative frameworks bring about higher levels of diversity in higher education systems.

It is along these lines that, in this book, we intend to develop an instrument for classifying higher education institutions. Assuming that institutional diversity in higher education systems (differences between institutions) can be stimulated by heterogeneous environments and by a variety in the norms and values expressed by specific types of institutions, we will suggest an instrument that is able to create transparency of diversity.

References

Aldrich, H.E. (1979). *Organizations and Environments*. Englewood Cliffs, NJ: Prentice-Hall.

Birnbaum, R. (1983). *Maintaining Diversity in Higher Education*. San Francisco, CA: Jossey-Bass.

Campbell, D.T. (1965). Variation and selective retention in socio-cultural evolution. In: H.R. Barringer, G.I. Blanksten & R.W. Mack (Eds.), *Social Change in Developing Areas*. Cambridge: Schenkman.

Clark, B.R. (1978). United States. In: J.H. van de Graaf, B.R. Clark, D. Furth, D. Goldschmidt & D. Wheeler (Eds.), *Academic Power: Patterns of Authority in Seven National Systems*. New York: Praeger.

Clark, B.R. (1983). *The Higher Education System*. Berkeley/Los Angeles, CA: University of California Press.

Coleman, J.S. (1990). *Foundation of Social Theory*. Cambridge: Harvard University Press.

DiMaggio, P.J. & Powell, W.W. (1983). The iron cage revisited: institutional isomorphism and collective rationality in organizational fields. *American Sociological Review* 48, 147–60.

Durkheim, E. (1893). *The Division of Labor in Society*. New York: The Free Press.

Fox, W. (1993). Higher education policy in California. In: L. Goedegebuure, F. Kaiser, P. Maassen, L. Meek, F. van Vught & E. de Weert (Eds.), *Higher Education Policy: An International Comparative Perspective* (pp. 49–82). Oxford: Pergamon.

Hannan, M.T. & Freeman, J. (1977). The population ecology of organizations. *American Journal of Sociology* 82, 929–64.

Hannan, M.T. & Freeman, J. (1989). *Organizational Ecology*. Cambridge: Harvard University Press.

Hawley, A.H. (1986). *Human Ecology; A Theoretical Essay*. Chicago, IL: University of Chicago Press.

Huisman, J. (1995). *Differentiation, Diversity and Dependency in Higher Education*. Utrecht: Lemma.

Huisman, J., Meek, L. & Wood, F. (2007). Institutional diversity in higher education: a cross-national and longitudinal analysis. *Higher Education Quarterly*, 61(4), 563–77.

Maassen, P.A.M. & Potman, H.P. (1990). Strategic decision making in higher education, an analysis of the new planning system in Dutch higher education. *Higher Education* 20, 393–410.

Meek, V.L. (1991). The transformation of Australian higher education: from binary to unitary system. *Higher Education* 21, 461–94.

Merton, R. (1968). *Social Theory and Social Structure*. New York: The Free Press.

Morgan, G. (1986). *Images of Organization*. London: Sage.

Morphew, Chr.C. (2006). *Conceptualizing Change in the Institutional Diversity of US Colleges and Universities*. International Centre for Higher Education Management. University of Georgia, Mimeo.

Neave, G. (1979). Academic drift: some views from Europe. *Studies in Higher Education* 4(2), 143–59.

Parsons, T. (1966). *Societies: Evolutionary and Comparative Perspectives*. Englewood Cliffs, NJ: Prentice-Hall.

Parsons, T. & Platt, G.M. (1973). *The American University*. Cambridge: Harvard University Press.

Pfeffer, J. & Salancik, G.R. (1978). *The External Control of Organizations, A Resource Dependence Perspective*. New York: Harper & Row.

Rhoades, G. (1990). Political competition and differentiation in higher education. In: J.C. Alexander & P. Colony (Eds.), *Differentiation Theory and Social Change*. New York: Columbia University Press.

Riesman, D. (1956). *Constraint and Variety in American Education*. Lincoln, NE: University of Nebraska Press.

Skolnik, M.L. (1986). Diversity in higher education: the Canadian case. *Higher Education in Europe* 11, 19–32.

Teichler, U. (2007a). The changing patterns of higher education systems in Europe and the future tasks of higher education research. In: European Science Foundation (Ed.), *Higher Education Looking Forward: Relations Between Higher Education and Society* (pp. 79–103). Strasbourg: European Science Foundation.

Teichler, U. (2007b). *Higher Education Systems, Conceptual Frameworks, Comparative Perspectives, Empirical Findings*. Rotterdam: Sense.

Trow, M. (1979). *Élite and Mass Higher Education: American Models and European Realities*. Stockholm: National Board of Universities.

Chapter 2
Diversity in European Higher Education: Historical Trends and Current Policies

Jeroen Huisman and Frans van Vught

2.1 Introduction

Europe and its universities have a strong and long-standing relationship. Over the centuries European universities have contributed significantly to the social, economic and cultural development of Europe. The very existence of the European universities reflects one of the most central dimensions of the "idea of Europe". Particularly from the age of the Enlightenment on, European universities became the institutional home of modernity and rationality. When, as Kant said, Europe broke out of its "self-imposed tutelage" during the Enlightenment, modernity became a fundamental European invention and modern science lay at the heart of that modernisation process. Rationality and the corresponding attitude to science and technology became essential and decisive elements of European identity. "Since Europe became Europe in its own eyes, science has been held up as its image and it emblem" (Daston 2005, p. 30).

Over time, European universities have changed considerably. Yet they also remained the central European institutions of reason, knowledge, criticism and learning. Plato's Academy was a centre of dialogue and critical enquiry. The medieval universities were open, self-governing communities of scholars. The "liberal university" of Cardinal John Newman was an institution for independent intellectual self-empowerment. And Wilhelm von Humboldt's proposals for the establishment of the University of Berlin were first of all aimed at preventing the search for knowledge being corrupted by social forces (Barnett 1990; De Ridder-Symoens 1992, 1996; Nybom 2003).

Through time, Nyborn = Nybom European universities have also regularly shown their "Europeanness". Although Plato's Academy was not the large community of students and teachers that we nowadays associate with the concept of the university, it was an open institution. Similarly, the medieval universities are known to have attracted scholars and *Wanderstudenten* from all over Europe. Helped by the fact that lectures were normally delivered in Latin, students and teachers moved easily from one university to the other, from Coimbra to Vilnius or from Uppsala to Salerno (Burke 2006, p. 237). In the sixteenth and seventeenth centuries many universities provided temporary academic homes for European scholars without consideration for national frontiers. Until the eighteenth century the European university was a European institution, reflecting European values of intellectual freedom and of a borderless academic community.

The rise of territorial states largely brought an end to these European academic peregrinations. In the eighteenth and nineteenth centuries, newly-emerging national states fostered their unity along the lines of a strong and homogeneous cultural identity, forcing universities into national frameworks. The effect was a "nationalisation" of science and (higher) education. European universities received their core funding from the Nation States, with an assumption that they were to train the cadres for the national civil services and contribute to the new national cultural identities, underpinning the nation-building processes. As a consequence, European universities nowadays are still largely national rather than European institutions. However, we may also be on the verge of a new phase of academic "Europeanness".

In this chapter we will discuss the diversity of European higher education. We will (briefly) examine the history of that diversity. We will describe the new emerging European policy contexts, both at the supranational and (in some cases) the national level, and we will present the current situation regarding institutional diversity in European higher education.

2.2   A History of Diversity in European Higher Education

A brief exploration of the centuries of European higher education history shows that the concept of diversity can be helpful in describing the general development of European higher education.

In the Middle Ages the medieval universities jointly formed an early European higher education system. Although they were in many ways very different, medieval universities were largely similar in terms of their missions. "the sixty or so universities of the medieval West were ... extremely various as regards their numbers, their intellectual orientations, their social role and the institutions themselves.... Nevertheless ... the universities had, at least in ideal terms, a universalist vocation" (Verger 1992, p. 45, 41).

Early Modern Europe (1500–1800) brought about a growing diversification of types of higher education institutions. According to Frijhoff three major types of universities can be distinguished, showing different missions and profiles:

- "Universities in the strict sense of the term ... recognised or legitimised by the *de facto* supreme authority in the territory, by its granting the rights to award degrees."
- "Teaching academics, higher or illustrious schools ... which could claim university status but had not obtained all its privileges, especially that of awarding degrees."
- "Colleges, teaching ... in the form of propaedeutic classes for university entrance or merely as an elementary form of higher education" (Frijhoff 1996, p. 68, 69).

Modern times in Europe (1800–) are first of all characterised by the rise of the Nation State, a process which has continued throughout the twentieth and into the early twenty-first centuries. As Davies notes: "of the sovereign states on the map of Europe in 1993, four had been formed in the sixteenth century, four in the seventeenth, two in the eighteenth, seven in the nineteenth, and no fewer than the thirty-six in the twentieth" (Davies 1997, p. 456). As mentioned earlier, the rise of the Nation State has produced the "nationalisation" of European higher education, creating higher education systems and institutions that were to meet the needs of the modern state. "The political culture represented by the nation demanded cultural domestication and social standardisation.... The university therefore took on the society-building role of providing a national education" (Henningsen 2006, p. 98).

The historical trends in diversity in European higher education show, on the one hand, a development from a broad European system to a set of national systems and, on the other hand, a certain diversification in terms of institutional missions and profiles, i.e. a process creating horizontal diversity (see Chapter 1).

Regarding this latter trend no clear information is available on the actual diversity of institutional missions and profiles in the various national higher education systems in Europe other than that provided in a formal, often legal sense. We may assume that a certain level of institutional diversity exists in many national European higher education systems. However, such an institutional diversity is more often based on regulation than on the actual characteristics or performances of the institutions involved.

Regarding the first trend, both the recent Bologna process and European Union (EU) policy initiatives (see below) have brought about a new pan-European approach to higher education. However, in these new European-wide approaches to higher education (both in the Bologna and EU contexts) the issue of the diversity of institutional missions and profiles has so far hardly been addressed. A major challenge for modern European higher education still appears to be to understand – and make transparent – its diversity.

2.3   Emerging European Policy Contexts

The establishment of the first European community treaties in the 1950s marks the beginning of the current European Union approach to higher education and research. In particular, the treaty creating the European Economic Community (EEC), signed in Rome in 1957, has been important: Article 235 of this treaty was the primary source of the EU's research policy.

Higher education has for a long time been "taboo" as an object of EU policy (Neave 1984, p. 6). Although some activities were developed at a European level during the 1970s (in particular in the field of vocational training), it took until the second half of the 1980s before the first EU policy initiatives appeared. The first EU programmes (such as Comett, Erasmus, Lingua and Tempus) were all proposed within a very short time and had a major input on the development of the European policy domain of higher education, triggering a European policy context in higher education, and resulting in a "qualitative and quantitative leap forward for community cooperation" (European Communities 2006, p. 109).

Also since the 1980s the EU research policy domain has been fully developed. The Single European Act (1987) and the Maastricht Treaty (1992) created important foundations for EU policy on research and technological development. Key to the development have been the Framework Programmes (FPs), the multi-annual research prioritisation and funding instruments that operate as medium-term planning tools for EU research strategy. The Framework Programmes have been growing in size and importance over the years and have developed into the major policy instrument of the European Research Area (ERA).

The European Research Area was created in 2000 when EU government leaders decided on their "Lisbon strategy". Wanting to create the "European knowledge society", they agreed on the ERA as a context to integrate national research policies, to encourage cooperation between researchers at the European level and to stimulate the links between universities and industry. The European Commission argued that European research represents a jigsaw of often very different national policies and that a genuine European approach to research was needed. The compartmentalisation, dispersion and duplication of research needed to decrease. Critical mass of human technological and financial resources had to be stimulated (European Commission 2002). The 6th (2002–2006) and 7th (2007–2013) Framework Programmes were designed and implemented to address these priorities.

In 2007 the idea of the ERA was developed further. In the face of increasing globalisation and new socio-economic challenges, EU research must improve its effectiveness and efficiency, argued the Commission. More public and private investments are needed and stronger links with other EU policies called for. According to the Commission the ERA must comprise six features:

1. An adequate flow of competent researchers with high levels of mobility among institutions, disciplines, sectors and countries
2. World-class research infrastructures, accessible to all
3. Excellent research institutions engaged in public–private cooperation, involved in clusters and communities, and attracting human and financial resources
4. Effective knowledge sharing between the public and private sectors and with the public at large
5. Well-coordinated research programmes and priorities and
6. The opening of the ERA to the world (European Commission 2007)

As with EU research policy, the EU treaties of the 1990s formed further important milestones for the higher education policy context. The Maastricht Treaty (1992) created for the first time a legal basis for EU higher education policy initiatives. The Treaty of Amsterdam (1997) put this in the broader context of the European knowledge society. The Treaty of Nice (2001) concluded that the European Union has a role to play in this policy domain that is complementary to the responsibilities of the Member States.

After 2000, higher education moved from the margins to the centre of EU policy-making concerns (Shaw 1999, p. 556; Corbett 2005, p. 11). One major policy initiative was the Socrates programme. After a first phase (1995–1999), the second phase of this programme (2000–2006) supported European cooperation in areas ranging from schools to higher education, and from new technologies to adult learning. The higher education sector of the programme continued the older Action Scheme on Mobility (the Erasmus programme, established in 1987) and the European Credit Transfer System (ECTS, introduced in 1989). In 2003 the first Erasmus Mundus programme (2004–2008) was presented as a response to the challenges faced by European higher education in a globalising world.

Inspired by the well-known EU 2000 Lisbon ambitions (to making Europe "the most competitive and dynamic knowledge-based economy in the world", European Council 2000), in 2003 the integrated Lifelong Learning programme (2007–2013) was proposed. The general objectives of this programme are to contribute to the development of the EU as an advanced knowledge society, and to foster cooperation and mobility between the EU's education and training systems. For higher education the aims are to reinforce the contribution of higher education to the European process of innovation and to support the creation of the European Higher Education Area (EHEA) (European Commission 2003a, b).

The ambition to create a "European Higher Education Area" had been formulated in another, broader, policy context a few years before. In 1998 the education ministers of France, Germany, Italy and the United Kingdom had agreed on the harmonisation of their higher education systems in the Sorbonne declaration. This declaration proved to be a quantum leap in the development of European higher education policy (Witte 2006, p. 124). As a follow-up, in the Bologna declaration (1999), 29 ministers formulated their wish to construct a European Higher Education Area, to promote mobility and employability and to increase the compatibility and comparability of Europe's higher education systems. The Bologna process became a major higher education policy context at a European-wide scale. In 2008 46 European (and other) countries were involved in this process, jointly developing a powerful intergovernmental policy-framework for European higher education. However, although often referred to as an important strength of European higher education, institutional diversity has played so far an ambiguous role in this policy context.

Both the EU and the (broader) Bologna policy contexts address European higher education and research at the supranational level (Van Vught 2009). For the first time since the rise of the Nation States, the twenty-first century appears to bring a renewed interest in the European-wide approach to these fields. In the higher education policy contexts the structural convergence of the various national systems is one of the major foci of attention. Increasing compatibility and comparability are the crucial objectives, but the importance of the diversity of European higher education is also regularly emphasised.

The Bologna Declaration stressed that comparability and compatibility should be realised within the context of national legislative competences, "taking full respect of the diversity of cultures, languages, national education systems and of university autonomy". But here the ambiguity creeps in: the declaration aims at structural convergence, but respects existing national diversities. The question emerging from this is whether attempts to converge go against or might clash with national competences. As such, clear-cut answers to the questions around institutional diversity are not offered by the Bologna documents. The Bergen Communiqué for instance stresses (again) that "[w]e must cherish our rich heritage and cultural diversity in contributing to a knowledge society" (Bergen Communiqué 2005). From the document it is far from clear which aspects of diversity are worthwhile to pursue and which are not, beyond general notions as language and cultural diversity.

The European Commission, in the context of the Lisbon ambitions, takes a slightly different slant to the issue. Instead of structural convergence, it takes institutional diversity as the point of departure: "The European university landscape … is characterised by a high degree of heterogeneity which is reflected in organisation, governance and operating conditions, including the status and conditions of employment and recruitment of teaching staff and researchers." Actors involved in European higher education should attempt to "organise that diversity within a more coherent and compatible European framework" (European Commission 2005, pp. 4–5). Also in a 2005 communication, the value of diversity is acknowledged up front: "There are deficiencies stemming from insufficient differentiation. Most universities tend to offer the same monodisciplinary programmes and traditional methods geared towards the same group of academically best-qualified learners … but Europe has too few centres of world-class excellence and universities are not encouraged to explain the specific value of what they produce for learners and society" (European Commission 2005, pp. 3–4). But despite raising the problem of a lack of diversity, the Commission at the same time, argues that there are limits to diversity: "European higher education is and needs to remain diverse with respect to languages, culture, systems and traditions. At the same time, sufficient compatibility between the different national regulations is indispensable in order to avoid breeding confusion rather than adding opportunities for citizen choice and mobility" (European Commission 2005, p. 6).

In sum, two supranational policy contexts (EU policies and the Bologna process) both support the idea of institutional diversity. But this support appears to be conditional. First, the policy documents are in favour of "organised diversity", thus setting some boundaries to institutional variety. Second, the policy documents are rather vague when it comes to specifying which elements of diversity are appreciated. It would not be too far-fetched to conclude that institutional diversity is appreciated as long as it does not go against the need for convergence of the fragmental European higher education system.

In the following sections we explore the effects of the emerging European policy contexts on the institutional diversity of European higher education and we try to assess the current situation regarding this diversity. We will do so, by first sketching the general trend across signatory countries along the Bologna action lines (building on Huisman 2008, 2009) and then by assessing the general diversity effects of the EU policies of research and higher education (building on Van Vught 2009). Next we will pay attention to some country examples to illustrate the particular dynamics at the level of some higher education systems. Finally we will formulate our overall conclusions.

2.4   Diversity in the Bologna Process

If we take the findings from recent comparative research projects regarding the state of the art with respect to the Bologna process together (Crosier et al. 2007; Eurydice 2005; Huisman et al. 2006; Reichert & Tauch 2005; Witte 2006), the following picture emerges. All studies confirm that there is some convergence among the signatory countries, particularly when it comes to the structure of the degree systems. That is, in most countries structural regulations and conditions are in place concerning the degree structure (two or three cycles), the Diploma Supplement, a credit transfer system, a qualifications framework and a quality assurance system. Countries have taken up the Bologna process and implemented many of its elements. But it is important to mention that this does not imply a full convergence. Various studies on the Bologna process have taught us that there can be a considerable gap between the intentions set out in the Bologna documents and the reality at the shop-floor level within higher education institutions (e.g. Gornitzka 2006). Various factors contribute to this gap: national policy-makers adjust the Bologna objectives and instruments to fit the particular national context, interest groups within the system have their input in the further operationalisation of the Bologna agenda at the national level, and at the institutional level it is up to institutional leaders, managers and academics to further substantiate the Bologna elements at the operational level. Hence, issues of policy "translation", willful influence on or hindrance of the implementation have a considerable impact on what actually happens in reality.

The complete answer to the question of convergence would therefore be "yes, but …". We illustrate this by looking in a bit more detail at some of the Bologna elements: the three-cycle structure, the Diploma Supplement and quality assurance.

Regarding the three-cycle structure, the Eurydice report (Eurydice 2007, p. 15) is correct in stating that "[a]t the start of the 2006/07 academic year, the three-cycle structure was in place in virtually all signatory countries." But it is also correct to state that a huge variety of models looms behind the convergence towards the three-cycle structure. The following table (Table 2.1) illustrates this variety for engineering programmes (Huisman et al. 2006, p. 36).

In a similar vein, the Diploma Supplement has been introduced in most of the countries. But there are still considerable differences across the countries, when it comes to the actual implementation: the Eurydice report states that in 2006/07 the Diploma Supplement was to be issued for all programmes in all institutions in half of the signatory countries. If the Diploma Supplement is issued, it takes place in a variety of ways, ranging from automatic and free of charge to on request and/or not free of charge. Also the language of the Diploma Supplement varies considerably, although the majority of countries issue the supplement (at least) in English (Eurydice 2007, pp. 29–32).

Table 2.1 Structure of cycles in engineering in Bologna countries (From Huisman et al. 2006, p. 36)

Structure	Country
3 + 2	Croatia, Czech Republic, Latvia, Romania, Germany (and 3.5 + 1.5), Hungary, Italy, Belgium, The Netherlands, Norway, Denmark, Iceland
4 + 1	Bulgaria, Malta
4 + 2	Turkey, Cyprus, Poland, Lithuania
Varying 3/4 + 1/2	Slovakia, Slovenia
2-cycle + undivided	UK, Ireland, Portugal
Moving to 2-cycle	Spain
No 2-cycle	France, Estonia, Sweden Austria, Finland, Greece

The last example concerns the action line of promoting European cooperation in quality assurance. In most countries national (or regional) agencies emerged to take up or have been assigned a role in quality assurance and control (Costes et al. 2008). And, indeed, various stakeholders (staff, management, students, employers) are involved in the quality assurance mechanisms. And yes, in the processes there is reliance on self-assessment and peer review. It can be assumed that the issuing of the European Standards and Guidelines and its underlying four-stage process (autonomy and independence of procedures and methods from government and institutions; self-assessment; external assessment by peer-review and site visits; publication of a report) have played and will play a role in the convergence process (Costes et al. 2008, pp. 44–47). At the same time, behind the general patterns, again, a myriad of variations can be found. These variations relate to the stress on quality control versus quality improvement, the roles of the various stakeholders in quality assurance and control, the level of analysis: programme and/or institutional level, and the specific tools at hand to carry out quality checks (see also Schwarz & Westerheijden 2004).

2.5 Diversity Effects of EU Policies

It may be too early to assess the effects of EU policies on the institutional diversity of European higher education. However, it can be argued that, generally speaking, the Lisbon ambitions clearly have triggered the wish to reinforce higher education's contribution to an integrated EU innovation strategy.

The EU research policy has a clear impact on European universities. The 6th and 7th Framework Programmes are among the largest R&D funding programmes in the world and provide vital opportunities for universities with limited research funding. In addition, for many universities the EU funding for collaborative research is a key element in their pursuit of international academic repute. In the context of research, there is a growing importance of the supranational EU policy echelon and a slowly increasing alignment between the EU policies and those of the member states. The EU research policy challenges European universities to increase their quality and reputation and to act at a global scale. European universities are being stimulated to respond to the growing international academic competition and to contribute to economic growth and social cohesion.

In the higher education policy context, the EU calls for a "modernisation strategy". According to the European Commission, European higher education is too traditional, too egalitarian and has too little world-class excellence. It is too fragmented in small and medium-sized subsystems with national regulations and languages, too insulated from industry, too dependent on the Nation States, inefficient and inflexible; and it is overregulated and underfunded. The European Commission wants European higher education institutions to become more attractive, increase their academic quality, intensify their relationships with business and industry, strengthen their human resources and compete internationally. The EC sees the diversity of European higher education as a strength but also suggests that this diversity needs to be combined with increased compatibility (European Commission 2005, 2006).

As a result of the EU's higher education and research policy focus the "social contract" between society and European higher education appears to be changing. In their educational programmes higher education institutions are urged to develop closer links with industry and society at large. In their research programmes they are prompted not only to address knowledge creation but also knowledge diffusion processes. "There are now much more explicit and direct expectations that, in return for public funding, universities ... should endeavor to deliver greater and more direct benefits to society" (Martin 2003, p. 25).

In addition, the overall governance model of European higher education institutions also appears to be changing. The move to more accountability has brought with it recognition of stakeholders' needs and interests, and hence the acceptance by higher education institutions of their social embeddedness and their relationships with and dependencies on various societal organisations. The result appears to be the emergence of a new, multi-stakeholder governance model with multiple funding sources, a stronger focus on autonomy combined with accountability, and a pressure to deliver innovation-relevant outcomes.

However, the effects in terms of institutional diversity are still hard to access. The EU policy ambition appears to be to combine diversity with compatibility, and to create an integrated European higher education system that can become a competitor to the dominant US system. In this integrated system a diversity of institutional roles and missions can possibly be seen as an important characteristic, or even as a condition to combine global academic competitiveness with socio-economic relevance and regional impact. But so far, the EU policy programmes remain relatively quiet, giving the impression that institutional diversity is not a major issue in an EU policy context.

Nevertheless, there appear to be two diversity effects of the EU *research* policy in particular that deserve attention. Both may be unintended "by-products" of EU policy, but both are real and increasingly visible.

The first of these two effects can be described as the academic stratification of the overall European higher education system, a process of increasing vertical diversity (see Chapter 1). This effect is the combined result of the changing participation processes of the European higher education institutions in the research Framework Programmes (FPs) and the occurrence of a counterproductive consequence of the reinforcement policy regarding the interaction between higher education and industry. With regard to the latter, it has been noted that past success in the FPs appears to be an indicator for successful future participation in these programmes (David and Keely 2003). What appears to be happening is the occurrence of the well-known Matthew Effect. Research groups that have been successful in obtaining funding appear to increase their chances of getting funds in the future as well (Geuna 1999, p. 117). The other process is the counterproductive effect of the EU's push towards closer links between higher education and industry. It appears that particularly those higher education institutions in a relatively weak financial position are increasingly forced to accept industrial funding for often routine contract research. Faced with the impossibility of charging the real research costs, these institutions are often confronted with a further weakening of their financial situation and a decrease in their capacity to undertake academic research. (Geuna 1999). The combined outcome of both processes is an increasing differentiation between academically and financially stronger institutions and weaker institutions, and hence a growing vertical diversity in the overall European higher education system.

The second unintended effect is a growing regional diversification in European higher education. This appears to be the outcome of three interrelated processes emerging from the EU research and innovation policies (Frenken et al. 2008). The first is the preference of researchers in "excellent regions" to collaborate with each other, rather than with colleagues in lagging regions. The EU research policy appears to stimulate the concentration of talent in the richer and academically better-equipped regions of Europe. Lagging regions find it difficult to participate in successful European research networks and appear to have to pass a threshold of quality and size before they can do so. Secondly, the EU policy objective of free movement of people appears to not only lead to an increased mobility of researchers but also to the concentration of talent in a selected number of excellent regions. The most talented researchers compete for the positions at the most prestigious universities, rendering it difficult for the lagging regions to retain talent within their borders. Thirdly, the sectoral structure of the poorer European regions is usually characterised by a dominance of low-tech and medium-tech activities that do not fit the thematic priorities of EU research policy. The FPs almost exclusively concern high-tech sectors, thus creating a situation in which the research subsidies are becoming concentrated in the richer regions. The result is an unintended but nevertheless real effect of regional diversification. The geography of European higher education and research is changing from one based on the priority of national borders into one based on the clustering of talent. Wealthier regions are increasingly able to profit from the general European innovation policy, while poorer regions are left with the resources of the cohesion policy. This process also appears to lead to a growing vertical diversity in Europe's higher education system. In wealthier regions the academic reputation of higher education institutions increases, leaving poorer regions with the academically weaker institutions.

Both processes, of academic stratification and regional diversification, are diversity effects of the EU's higher education and, especially, research policies. Both processes are indications of an increasing institutional diversity in the European higher education and research areas. But both also are largely unintended "by-products" of policies that so far have not clearly and intentionally addressed the issue of diversity in European higher education. It appears that the time has come to do just that.

2.6   Diversity in National Higher Education Systems

The analysis above has shown the variety across Europe when it comes to the actual implementation of elements of the Bologna process and to the effects of the EU higher education and research polices. With regard to the Bologna process one might suggest that diversity has increased: in many countries old and new structures and procedures still co-exist, which increases – at least temporarily – the variety within those systems. However, it would also be safe to argue that when the countries are beyond the transition stage, there is some structural homogeneity across these countries, but much micro-level variety (sometimes hidden diversity) behind these communalities. With respect to the EU context diversification effects appear to result from especially the application of the powerful EU research policy instruments (the FPs). Here the suggestion can be that diversity is increasing, perhaps not as an outcome of intended policy but nevertheless as an emerging reality. However, this growing diversity mainly regards institutional and regional differentiation along the more or less traditional lines of academic performance and reputation (vertical diversity). Differentiation in terms of institutional missions and profiles (horizontal diversity) has so far not been addressed in the EU policy context.

In order to add to our general picture of the current diversity in European higher education we now focus on the national level of higher education in Europe. What are the recent developments with respect to diversity in the national European higher education systems? We take the examples of five countries, sketching the most important trends in each of these countries pertaining to institutional diversity.

2.6.1   France[1]

The French higher education system is very diverse and thus often difficult to understand for external observers. The term "university" is used for institutions allowed to deliver the degrees DEUG (2 years after the *baccalauréat*), the *licence*, the *maîtrise* and the DEA (research oriented) or DESS (more profession oriented).

---

[1] We thank Christine Musselin, Centre de Sociologie des Organisations (Sciences-Po and Centre National de Recherche Scientifique) for drafting the section on France.

Developed as degree-granting institutions, French universities only relatively recently – compared to most other continental higher education systems – were considered as research institutions. To cope with the low levels of research activity of universities, many national research centres have been created. Moreover, French universities are not considered as the most prestigious training places. The so-called *grandes écoles* have become the leaders in the training of the French elites and top executives in engineering, business and management and public administration. Whereas the universities are open to all *baccalauréat* holders, the *grandes écoles* are highly selective training institutes; students prepare through 2-year *classes préparatoires*. A few of the *grandes écoles* are research-intensive, but others only recently became so. On top of the university/*grandes écoles* divide, there are two degrees leading to a professional higher education degree. The first one (DUT, *diplôme universitaire de technologie*) is delivered by the IUTs (*Instituts Universitaire de Technologie*) which are specific entities within the universities. The other one, the BTS (*brevet de technicien supérieur*) is delivered in post-high school classes by private or public high school as a 2-year higher education degree. Graduates of the DUT and BTS programmes have access to the third university year (leading to the *licence*), implying a fair amount of flexibility across sectoral divides.

Apart from horizontal diversity in the system, addressed above, vertical diversity can be found as well, but only in the *grandes écoles* sector. Rankings for this sector were developed well before Bologna (but were mostly based on the level of wages earned by graduates). The dominant rationale for universities, however, was that university degrees (and therefore the degree-granting universities) were equivalent.

After Bologna most of the above-described boundaries are blurred, although the Bologna process has not been the main cause. In fact, universities were the only places to widely adopt the bachelor–master scheme. The IUT still deliver a specific degree in 2 years, the same holds true for the BTS and the *classes préparatoires*. The *grandes écoles* do not deliver bachelors but have their own masters. Nevertheless, different trends push for closer relationships between the universities and the *grandes écoles*. First, they both deliver a degree which has the same name (master) even if the legal status is different (national degrees at universities, institution-based degrees at *grandes écoles*). Second, some universities and *grandes écoles* offer co-masters. Third, the 2006 *Loi d'Orientation et de Programmation de la Recherche et de l'Innovation* allowed the creation of meta-structures called PRES (*Pôles d'enseignement supérieur et de recherche*) in which different institutions focusing on specific research activities can join and develop common activities such as graduate schools and research projects. In some of the PRES, universities and *grandes écoles* are involved, again favouring closer relationships between the two institutional groups. It has to be emphasised however, that collaboration across the sectors was visible before Bologna; the Bologna process has accelerated that cooperation (Musselin 2008).

A further trend, unrelated to the Bologna process, concerns the blurring divide between the universities and the national research institutions. The 2006 Research

Act and the 2007 University Act invite the universities to be strategic actors in research production and national research institutions are asked to redefine their role and their relations with the universities. As a result, there is an emerging trend towards converging missions between the different sectors and a concomitant increase in prestige of universities. At the same time, vertical diversity in the university sector is also increasing. First, with the introduction of 4-year contracts between each university and the Ministry from the beginning of the 1990s onwards and the preparation of strategic plans, there are clear incentives for universities to demonstrate what makes them different. Second, the current government develops a discourse on performance and excellence, emphasising the existence of differences among universities and the need to assess and differently reward this. Different forms of competition have been recently implemented. Universities with the "best" plans to improve their bachelor programmes and to reduce their drop-out rates have been identified. Universities have also been invited to compete for the best institutional project (partly based on scientific objectives and partly on campus development) in a contest called "Campus operation".

2.6.2 Germany

In Germany, we see a blurring of the boundaries between the *Fachhochschulen* and universities, because the former are – in the context of the Bologna process – now allowed to offer master's programmes as well. This change is not extremely radical, because the *Fachhochschulen* were already supposed to carry out (practice-oriented) research in the pre-Bologna period. As a consequence, the doctorate degree was not uncommon among *Fachhochschul* staff. In addition, the access routes between the two institutional types were not that clearly demarcated: for some *Fachhochschul* programmes, the entry rates for *Abitur* holders were higher than for the universities (Witte 2006, p. 160 and 370–376).

Some other developments regarding diversity are more striking. This was mainly due to the so-called *Exzellenzinitiative* launched in 2004. The then Minister Bulmahn announced a national competition among universities to support high-quality research and its international visibility, to support academic *Nachwuchs*, to strengthen cooperation across disciplinary boundaries and to strengthen international networking (Wissenschaftsrat 2008). How the idea emerged exactly is not totally clear from the literature, but it can be assumed that the EU policy context and particularly the ambitions of the Lisbon process played a considerable role. Fallon (2007, p. 57–58) also points at the fact that German policy-makers – in their search for solutions to problems around quantity (overloaded universities, high teacher to student ratios) and quality (lack of visible diversity) – increasingly looked at the US, a system characterised by explicit diversity, as an exemplary model. The government made a budget of €1.9 billion available for the period 2006–2010 and universities could propose initiatives in three areas: graduate schools (about 40 to be awarded), centres or clusters of excellence with international reputation (about 30 to be awarded), and full-scale institutional development plans towards excellent universities (about 10 to be awarded). The initiative was revolutionary in the sense that in German higher education, equality in opportunities for and treatment of all higher education institutions has been a long-standing hallmark of the system (Kehm & Pasternak 2008). There was an overwhelming amount of proposals (253 graduate school experiments; 280 excellence cluster proposals; and 47 excellence plans) (Fallon 2007). Decision-making has taken place only recently, 37 out of 88 universities were – in one way or another – prize-winners (Fallon 2008). The impact on the higher education system remains to be seen, but the attempt is there to bring more vertical differentiation to the landscape and the first signs are that this impact is strongly felt, both by winners and losers (Kehm & Pasternak 2008).

2.6.3 The Netherlands

Pre-Bologna, the Dutch higher education system was a clear example of a binary system of higher professional education (provided by *hogescholen*) and universities (Huisman & Kaiser 2001). The three distinctive features demarcating that boundary relate to formal access, the research function and the degrees awarded. The formal route to higher professional education is the 5-year senior general secondary education track (HAVO) and the formal secondary education route to universities is the 6-year pre-university track (VWO). Regarding the research function, universities are assumed – according to the national legislation – to carry out independent research and to prepare students for independent scientific work in an academic or professional setting. *Hogescholen* are supposed to offer theoretical instruction and to develop the skills required for practical application in a particular profession. In other words, universities carry out basic and applied research and *hogescholen* are allowed to do applied research. The demarcation with respect to the research function is reflected in the type of degrees awarded. *Hogescholen* offered 4-year bachelor degrees and universities offered master's (i.e. a 4–6-year integrated programme) and Ph.D. degrees. As will be understood, the two latter distinctions had an impact on the composition of staff at *hogescholen* and universities as well. The number of teachers at *hogescholen* with a Ph.D. was very small, certainly compared with the number of staff with a Ph.D. at the universities, where a Ph.D. generally is required for a long-term or tenured appointment at a university.

The current situation is much more dynamic and transparent than the relatively stable pre-Bologna situation. Universities and *hogescholen* have implemented the two-cycle system. For *hogescholen* this implied largely a change of terminology, but no comprehensive overhaul of the degree system. But, the *hogescholen* saw in the Bologna processes a window of opportunity to lobby for approval to offer (professional) master's degrees. To some extent, *hogescholen* already offered master's degrees, but these were co-operative efforts with UK universities on a kind of franchise basis and the number of programmes was limited. Obviously, the universities did not want to enter into competition with the *hogescholen* in the master's programme market and the Ministry of Education, Culture and Science had its reservations, particularly in terms of the financial consequences. A "solution" was found by proposing that the Ministry was willing to fund a master programme if the programme would be accredited by the Dutch/Flemish accreditation organisation (NVAO) and a *hogeschool* could convincingly argue – to the Ministry – that the programme would contribute significantly to the Dutch knowledge society. As a result of the decision, almost half of the *hogescholen* now offer a limited range of professional master programmes – in total a bit more than 100, compared to 900 masters at universities (2007 data) – most acknowledged and funded by the government.

A related development at the *hogescholen* was the emergence of a new personnel category (with a historical name): *lectors*. The idea of the lectorate was introduced to establish and maintain linkages and networks between the domains of (higher) education, the professions and applied research. Currently there are more than 400 *lectors*. One could see the emergence of the lectorate as a kind of professorship in applied research and thus an element of academic drift; it could equally be seen as an evitable development in a knowledge society, where all kinds of contributions to knowledge sharing and exchange are appreciated and a society in which boundaries between basic and applied research are becoming more and more blurred (see also Gibbons 1995 on mode 1 and mode 2 research).

In sum, through a variety of drivers the Dutch higher education landscape is changing considerably. Whereas the division of labour between *hogescholen* and universities used to be (relatively) clear-cut, the current situation is much fuzzier. *Hogescholen* offer master's programmes and call themselves "university" (of applied science). They also become more seriously involved in research of an applied nature. The Bologna agenda played a role in this development, in that the bachelor–master discussion in the Netherlands was a trigger for the *hogescholen* to claim the right to offer master's programmes. In addition, the EU policy context offers the attractive prospect of extra funding and international prestige to both universities and *hogescholen*.

2.6.4 Norway

In the mid-1990s the Norwegian college sector was reorganised, and the then largely vocationally-oriented colleges (about 100) were merged into 26 state colleges. From that period on, Norway has had a formal binary system of colleges and universities (including specialised university institutions), organised through unified legislation for both sectors. Kyvik (2008) argues that since then several aspects of academic drift can be observed, e.g. the vertical extension of teaching programmes at colleges (the offering of master's and Ph.D. degrees), the development of research activities at colleges, and colleges introducing an academic appointment and reward system. The case of Norway can be distinguished from the Dutch and German cases. First of all, there are hardly tendencies towards vertical diversity, although it is implicitly acknowledged that the University of Oslo is a high-quality research-intensive university with the most prestige and status. A second difference relates to the instruments in place to regulate sectoral boundaries. In the Netherlands and Germany, the government (still) maintains those boundaries through legislation, whereas the Norwegian government has put in place mechanisms to allow colleges to gain specialised status as either a university institution or university. The Norwegian Agency for Quality Assurance in Education (NOKUT) must approve the application for a change of status. Once NOKUT approves a case, the Ministry of Education and Research then makes the authoritative decision, but does not necessarily have to accept NOKUT's assessment. Criteria that play a role in this process are: the award of master's and Ph.D. degrees and successful master and Ph.D. graduations in a number of disciplines; meeting accreditation standards for the masters' and Ph.D. programmes; R&D production; research staff with formal qualifications; infrastructure for research activities, and well-established national and international academic networks (Stensaker 2004). Since the new regulations were put in place, three institutions (two former colleges and one former specialised university institution) have acquired full university status and there are applications pending. In addition, some colleges are considering merging to be able to make the transfer to university status easier. Concerns have been raised about processes of academic drift leading to a (too) homogeneous higher education system. Kyvik (2008, p. 187) states that "the development over the last two decades has shown gradually more emphasis on academic norms and values at the expense of traditional vocational and practice-related education" and "the binary system is eroding". Also an evaluation of NOKUT points in this direction, stating that the accreditation mechanisms may be too geared towards being or becoming a research-intensive higher education institution (Langfeldt et al. 2008) threatening the overall diversity of the system. An expert review (Stjernø Commission 2008) has concluded that the Norwegian system is too fragmented and scattered and suggests that the number of institutions (now about 35) should be brought back to eight to 10 larger institutions by 2020, with each new institution aiming to establish a specific, distinct profile in the Norwegian landscape. But national coordination and institutional cooperation would have to play an important role as well. How such plans – if implemented – would affect the higher education landscape (beyond the sheer number of institutions) is unclear.

The Norwegian case shows a binary system under pressure, because the regulations offer the opportunity for the emergence of cross-sectoral divides. The pressure particularly relates to academic drift. There are serious concerns about the preservation of diversity, but also about fragmentation and the large number of higher education institutions relative to the size and population of the country.

2.6.5   United Kingdom

In the UK EU policy initiatives and the Bologna process – despite UK involvement in its initiation – have not stirred much debate. Obviously, given that an undergraduate-graduate system was already in place and quality assurance institutionalised, there was not much left on the political agenda. Only recently has the question been raised as to whether the UK is too laid-back (Cemmell & Bekhradnia 2008 refer to a "spirit of aloofness") and point out that the UK's 1-year master programmes could be out of step with the intentions of other Bologna countries and that high master's fees for international students may put the UK at a disadvantage compared to other European countries offering similar programmes (many of which are delivered in English).

With respect to diversity, the issues at stake – tensions between sectors – do not differ much from those in Germany, Norway and the Netherlands, the big difference being that in the UK the formal binary system of universities and polytechnics was resolved in 1992. At present universities and former polytechnics are governed by similar regulations, quality assurance and funding mechanisms. The most important remaining divide between the two former sectors is the amount and quality of research carried out. The bulk of basic research is carried out by the research-intensive pre-1992 universities and the role of the former polytechnics is marginal. This situation is not due so much to political or institutional choices in the past decade, but largely to historical legacies. But exactly this legacy – or better the consequences of this in terms of a lack of equal research development capacities for the former polytechnics *vis-à-vis* the universities – is an ongoing point of debate. The formation of certain coalitions and interest groups around the research-teaching nexus can be seen as an example of a new process of differentiation emerging in the UK sector. The most research-intensive universities have formed the Russell Group to promote the interests of universities in which teaching and learning are undertaken within a culture of research excellence. The Russell Group of about 20 universities, set up in 1994, accounts for about two thirds of UK universities' research grants. At the other end of the spectrum of interest groups the University Alliance group can be found. Some 20 universities are members of this recently (2006) established group, consisting mainly of former polytechnics. Their primary objective is to bring about changes to the Research Assessment Exercise and teaching funding.

As important as these intra-university sector dynamics is what happens on the boundaries of the university and non-university sector. The latter sector consists of higher education colleges and further education colleges, together catering for about 20% of all higher education students. While these institutions have existed for decades and some for centuries, the current and past Labour governments (see, e.g. DfES 2003; Parry 2006) have emphasised the importance of these institutions in contributing to widening access and participation (towards a 50% participation rate). Foundation degrees – short-cycle degrees leading to an intermediate qualification, implemented in 2000 – to be provided through partnerships between further education colleges, higher education colleges and universities were seen as major instruments to achieve the objectives around access and participation. As another element of the package for widening participation and the stronger emphasis on excellent teaching, the government proposed to relax the rules for degree-awarding powers. In future, the title of university could be granted to an institution (private or public), without needing to have research degree-awarding powers. Since the launch of this policy, a number of non-university institutions have gained the title of university and a number of proposals are pending.

The formation of interest groups like the Russell Group and University Alliance may be an expression of increasing institutional diversity. But there is a problem regarding this process. One outstanding characteristic of the UK system is its steep hierarchy (despite a unitary system) of institutions. Institutions such as Oxford, Cambridge, Imperial College and University College London are known as prestigious world-class universities which are definitely in a different league when it comes to available resources (e.g. endowments), the tough entry selection, and – partly consequently – its output and performance. But given that in the context of this steep hierarchy, the focus is largely on prestige and status (with some attention to output indicators), there is a lack of transparency regarding what is actually behind the labels of prestige and status.

2.7 Conclusion

Generally speaking, it appears that from a cross-national and longitudinal perspective European higher education is in a state of flux. Analysis regarding the Bologna process shows that there is some system-level convergence around the core elements of this process. At the same time, we see many national and regional/local idiosyncrasies that make it difficult to conclude that a full harmonisation is taking place. There remains a large (sometimes hidden) micro-level variety behind the façade of the new structures and procedures.

Regarding the EU policy contexts, in particular the EU research policy appears to create diversity effects that may be unintended but are nevertheless becoming increasingly visible. On a European scale both a growing academic stratification and an increasing regional diversification appear to be emerging. These two processes of differentiation follow the traditional path of increasing diversity in terms of academic performance and reputation, thus creating a growing vertical diversity.

The five national higher education systems discussed in this chapter show that the landscapes are changing considerably at national level as well. In the Netherlands, Norway and the UK processes of academic drift are taking place at the boundaries of the sectors, partly as reaction to governmental policy initiatives. In France a convergence in missions between universities and research institutions is taking place and an increasing vertical diversity appear to be the trends in the university sector. In Germany a differentiation process is beginning to emerge from the *Exzellenzinitiative*, potentially resulting in an academic stratification process (vertical diversity) and eventually leading to a hierarchy similar to the one in UK higher education.

We conclude that the current situation regarding diversity in European higher education shows that the two sets of variables (mentioned at the end of Chapter 1) that are assumed to have an influence on differentiation processes in higher education systems, clearly appear to have an impact on the present European higher education system dynamics. Both the environmental conditions of higher education institutions (and particularly governmental policies, whether supranational or national) and the attraction of certain normative systems (particularly academic norms and values) appear to be highly relevant in the diversity dynamics of present-day European higher education. As the German case shows, at a national level governmental policies intended to create diversity are able to do so by means of shaping clearly different environmental conditions for different groups of institutions. On the other hand, governmental policies that allow the boundaries between categories of institutions to become blurred see the level of institutional diversity decrease. In these latter cases, the prestige of academic norms and values (often coupled with attractive funding conditions) leads to academic drift, creating a tendency towards uniformity and decreasing levels of horizontal diversity. At the supranational level the high level of uniformity of policy conditions (both in the Bologna process and in the EU contexts) implies that no direct differentiation effects can be expected to occur. However, the already existing differences in contextual and internal conditions of higher education institutions either appear to continue to exist (as is the case in the large micro-level diversity in the Bologna process) or are even being intensified (as is the case in the EU research policy context). In this sense especially the EU policy context is creating some unintended diversity effects of academic stratification and regional diversification, leading to increasing levels of vertical diversity.

Finally we can also conclude that the various differentiation (and homogenisation) processes taking place in Europe higher education lack transparency. It is becoming increasing difficult to discern what actually is to be found behind the label "university". Similarly, labels such as *hogescholen*, *Fachhochschulen*, and related names are increasingly covering a wide variety of institutional profiles. The only indicators that so far appear to play a role in the dynamics of diversity are those related to (academic) prestige and status. The diversification that is being triggered and amplified by national and supranational policies is that of prestige, creating an academic stratification process and a hierarchical ordering of institutions along the well-known lines of academic reputation. Such an approach clearly is inadequate to address the diversity of European higher education. If we really want to understand the dynamics in European higher education we need to increase the transparency of its diversity.

References

Barnett, R. (1990). *The Idea of Higher Education*. Buckingham: Open University Press.
Bergen Communiqué. (2005). The European Higher Education Area – achieving the goals. Bergen.
Burke, P. (2006). How to write a History of Europe, Europes, Eurasia. *European Review* 14(2), 233–239.
Cemmell, J. & Bekhradnia, B. (2008). *The Bologna Process and the UK's International Student Market*. Oxford: Higher Education Policy Institute.
Costes, N., Crozier, F., Cullen, P., Grifoll, J., Harris, N., Helle, E., et al. (2008). *Quality Procedures in the European Higher Education Area and Beyond – Second ENQA Survey*. Helsinki: European Association for Quality Assurance in Higher Education.

Corbett, A. (2005). *Universities and the Europe of Knowledge*. New York/Houndsmills/ Basingstoke/Hampshire: Palgrave McMillan.

Crosier, D., Purser, L. & Smidt, H. (2007). *Trends V: Universities Shaping the European Higher Education Area*. Brussels: EUA.

Daston, L. (2005). *The History of Science as European Self-Portraiture*. Premium Erasmianum Essay 2005. Amsterdam: Mart Spruijt.

Davies, N. (1997). *Europe, A History*. London: Pimlico.

David, P.A. & L.C. Keely (2003). The economics of scientific research coalitions, collaborative network formation in the presence of multiple funding agencies. In: A. Geuna, A.J. Salter & W.E. Steinmueller (Eds.), *Science and Innovation, Rethinking the Rationales for Funding and Governance* (pp. 251–308). Cheltenham: Edward Elgar.

De Ridder-Symoens, H. (Ed.). (1992, 1996). *A History of the University in Europe*, Vols. I and II. Cambridge: Cambridge University Press.

DfES. (2003). *The Future of Higher Education*. London: HMSO.

European Commission. (2002). *Toward a European Research Area*, COM (2002), 6, Brussels.

European Commission. (2003a). *Researchers in the European Research Area: One Profession, Multiple Careers*, COM (2003), 436, Brussels.

European Commission. (2003b). *The Role of Universities in the Europe of Knowledge*, COM (2003), 58.

European Commission. (2005). *Mobilising the Brainpower of Europe: Enabling Universities to Make Their Full Contribution to the Lisbon Strategy*, COM (2005), 152, Brussels.

European Commission. (2006a). *Time to Move up a Gear: The New Partnership for Growth and Jobs*, COM (2006), 30, Brussels.

European Communities. (2006b). *The History of European Cooperation in Education and Training, Europe in the Making – An Example*. Luxembourg: Office for Official Publication of the European Communities.

European Commission. (2007). *The European Research Area: New Perspectives*, Green Paper, COM (2007), 161, Brussels.

European Council. (2000). *European Council Presidency Conclusions*, 100/1/00, Lisbon.

Eurydice. (2005). *Focus on the Structure of Higher Education in Europe 2004/05. National Trends in the Bologna Process*. Brussels: Eurydice.

Eurydice. (2007). *Focus on the Structure of Higher Education in Europe 2006/07. National Trends in the Bologna Process*. Brussels: Eurydice.

Fallon, D. (2007). Germany and the United States, then and now: Seeking eminence in the research university. In: *The Crisis of the Publics Symposium, 26–27 March 2007* (pp. 55–67). University of California, Berkeley.

Fallon, D. (2008). Germany's "Excellence Initiative". *International Higher Education* 52 (Summer), 16–18.

Frenken, K., Hoekman, J. & van Oort, F. (2008). *Towards a European Research Area*. Rotterdam: NAI Publishers.

Frijhoff, W. (1996). Patterns. In: H. De Ridder-Symoens (Ed.). *A History of the University in Europe*, Vol. II (pp. 43–111). Cambridge: Cambridge Press.

Geuna, A. (1999). *The Economics of Knowledge Production: Funding and the Structure of University Research*. Cheltenham: Edward Elgar.

Gibbons, M. (1995). The university as an instrument for the development of science and basic research: The implications of mode 2 science. In: D.D. Dill & B. Sporn (Eds.), *Emerging Patterns of Social Demand and University Reform: Through a Glass Darkly* (pp. 90–104). Oxford: Pergamon.

Gornitzka, A. (2006). What is the use of Bologna in national reform? The case of Norwegian quality reform in higher education. In: V. Tomusk (Ed.), *Creating the European Area of Higher Education. Voices from the Periphery* (pp. 19–41). Dordrecht: Kluwer.

Henningsen, B. (2006). A joyful good-bye to Wilhelm von Humboldt: The German University and the Humboldtion ideals of *Einsamkeit* and *Freiheit*. In: G. Neave, K. Blückert & T. Nybom (Eds.), *The European Research University* (pp. 91–108). New York/Houndsmills/Basingstoke/ Hampshire: Palgrave McMillan.

Huisman, J. (2008). Shifting boundaries in higher education: Dutch *hogescholen* on the move. In: J.S. Taylor, J.B. Ferreira, M.d.L. Machado & R. Santiago (Eds.), *Non-university Higher Education in Europe* (pp. 147–167). Dordrecht: Springer.

Huisman, J. (2009). Institutional diversification or convergence? In: B. Kehm, J. Huisman & B. Stensaker (Eds.), *The European Higher Education Area: Perspectives on a Moving Target.* Rotterdam: Sense.

Huisman, J. & Kaiser, F. (2001). *Fixed and Fuzzy Boundaries in Higher Education. A Comparative Study of (Binary) Systems in Nine Countries.* The Hague: AWT.

Huisman, J., Witte, J. & File, J.M. (2006). *The Extent and Impact of Higher Education Curricular Reform Across Europe.* Enschede: CHEPS.

Kehm, B. & Pasternak, P. (2008, 24–27 August). *The German "Excellence Initiative" and its role in restructuring the national higher education landscape.* Paper presented at the 30th Annual EAIR Forum, Copenhagen, Denmark.

Kehm, B., Huisman, J. & Stensaker, B. (Eds.). (2009). *The European Higher Education Area: Perspectives on a moving target.* Rotterdam: Sense.

Kyvik, S. (2008). The non-university higher education sector in Norway. In: J.S. Taylor, J.B. Ferreira, M.d.L. Machado & R. Santiago (Eds.) Non-University Higher Education in Europe (pp 169–189). Dordrecht:Springer

Langfeldt, L., Harvey, L., Huisman, J., Westerheijden, D.F. & Stensaker B. (2008), Evaluation of NOKUT: NOKUTs national role. Oslo: NIFU-STEP

Martin, B.R. (2003). The changing social contract for science and the evolution of the university. In: A. Geuna, A.J. Salter & W.E. Steinmueller (Eds.), *Science and Innovation, Rethinking the Rationales for Funding and Governance* (pp. 7–29). Cheltenham: Edward Elgar.

Musselin, C. (2008). The side-effects of the Bologna Process on national institutional settings. In: A. Amaral, P. Maassen, C. Musselin & G. Neave(Eds.) European Integration and the Governance of Higher education and Research, The challenges and complexities of an emerging multi-level governance system. Dordrecht: Springer

Neave, G. (1984). *Education and the EEC.* London: Trentham Books.

Nybom, T. (2003). The Humboldt legacy: Reflections on the past, present and future of the European university. *Higher Education Policy* 16(2), 141–160.

Parry, G. (2006). Policy-participation trajectories in English higher education. *Higher Education Quarterly* 60(4), 392–412.

Reichert, S. & Tauch, C. (2005). *Trends IV: European Universities Implementing Bologna.* Brussels: EUA.

Schwarz, S. & Westerheijden, D.F. (Eds.). (2004). *Accreditation and Evaluation in the European Higher Education Area.* Dordrecht: Kluwer.

Shaw, J.B. (1999). From the margin to the centre: Education and Training Law and Policy from Casagrande to the 'Knowledge Society' In: P. Craig and G.de Burca (Eds.), *The Evolution of EU Law* (pp. 555–595). Oxford: Oxford University Press.

Stensaker, B. (2004). The blurring boundaries between accreditation and audit: the case of Norway. In: S. Schwarz & D.F. Westerheijden (Eds.) Accreditation and Evaluation in the European Higher Education Area (pp. 347–369). Dordrecht: Springer

Stjerno Commission (2008), Sett under Ett. Ny struktur i hoyere utdanning. Oslo: Norges offentlige utredninger

Van Vught, F.A. (2009). The Europe of knowledge. In: D.D. Dill & F.A. van Vught (Eds.), *National Innovation and the Academic Research Enterprise.* Baltimore, MD: Johns Hopkins University Press.

Verger, J. (1992). Patterns. In: H. De Ridder-Symoens (Ed.), *A History of the University in Europe,* Vol. I (pp. 35–76). Cambridge: Cambridge University Press.

Wissenschaftsrat. (2008). Exzellenzinitiative (http://www.wissenshaftsrat.de/exini_start.html)

Witte, J. (2006). *Change of Degrees and Degrees of Change, Comparing Adaptations of European Higher Education Systems in the Context of the Bologna Process.* Enschede: Centre for Higher Education Policy Studies, University of Twente.

Chapter 3
The Search for Transparency: Convergence and Diversity in the Bologna Process

Dirk Van Damme

3.1 Introduction

Building on preceding chapters, this chapter will focus on the national and European policies regarding convergence and diversity in higher education in the context of the Bologna Process. It will start with an analysis of the approaches to convergence and diversity in the Bologna Process, leading to the conclusion that the Bologna Process has been affected by a confusion between systemic convergence in the European Higher Education Area (EHEA) and institutional homogenisation. Subsequently, the argument is developed that the next phase in the Bologna Process (2010–2020) should address the issue of institutional diversity and develop policies to strengthen the European higher education system by promoting and fostering evidence-based institutional diversity. Convergence will still be the driving force in the Bologna Process, but is not contradictory to increasing institutional diversity; on the contrary, systemic convergence and transparency create a favourable environment for institutional diversification. But in turn, increasing diversity also needs new tools for evidence-based transparency in which diversity can be made visible and comprehensible.

3.2 Convergence in the Bologna Process

After almost 10 years, even its most ardent sceptics and opponents will recognise that the Bologna Process has been the driver of a remarkably successful political process of reform in European higher education. As described in the preceding chapter, after decades of important, pioneering but purely voluntary forms of cooperation in the context of EU programmes such as Erasmus, Socrates, Leonardo, Tempus and others (Papatsiba 2006), the 29 ministers signing the Bologna Declaration in 1999 started a process of more structural convergence, which should lead to the establishment of a European Higher Education Area (EHEA) by 2010. Although the reform process was not formally binding by European legal instruments (sometimes leading to allegations of the "undemocratic" nature of the process) and based upon inter-, not supra-governmental steering, the Bologna Process has been very powerful in influencing national policy developments.

Several mutually reinforcing factors contributed to this: after many years of relatively spontaneous internationalisation policies at institutional and national levels, the ground had been made fertile for more structural reform aiming at the establishment of a truly integrated European space of higher education; the bottom-up structure of the reform process, with the institutions' organisations, student representatives and quality assurance networks actively involved, guaranteed an inclusive policy process, leading to a unique political governance structure; the "soft" nature of the intergovernmental steering, linked to the emerging popularity of notions of "soft government" and the "open method of coordination", left sufficient room for national policy development, to the idea of "subsidiarity" and to the trusted roles of stakeholders and social partners. All this did not weaken the reform process, on the contrary: the Bologna Process can be seen as one of the most successful recent examples of transnational reform.

Yet, not much is known about the real impact of the Bologna Process on national policy developments. "To put it differently, we still do not know to what degree higher education policy is converging in the course of the Bologna Process, and what exactly the reasons for national differences in convergence effects are" (Heinze & Knill 2008). The mechanisms which made the Bologna Process effective and the factors which can explain its efficacy still have to be researched. The Bologna Process appears to have operated as a kind of transnational communication, combining guidelines, which were produced "bottom-up" but received ministerial approval and were then interpreted as relatively binding by the countries, leading to information exchanges involving various levels of decision-makers. This complex process of communication produced both what political scientists call "delta convergence" (compliance to an authoritative model defined by an international organisation or forerunner) and "sigma convergence" (decreasing variation by similar national policies) (Heinze & Knill 2008). Guidelines and objectives set by the ministerial meetings and communiqués were influential (especially the Bergen Communiqué of 2005), but were accompanied by parallel processes of information exchange and standards setting during numerous meetings involving a large group of supporters. These supporters acted as ambassadors in institutional networks and national policy development interactions. Despite encountering resistance in some countries (paradoxically especially the big countries signing the Sorbonne Declaration a year before), among some stakeholders (more specifically certain sectors of national student bodies and some trade unions) and from the rank and file of some institutions, the Bologna reforms gained a sense both of inevitability and of being beneficial. Its critics sometimes complained that the reforms were seen as sacrosanct and thus difficult to oppose.

All this would have been impossible without the strong policy message of convergence and transparency that steered the reform. This message was conveyed with great conviction and persuasiveness by policy-makers and the level of ambassadors in institutions, organisations and networks. Those listening were highly receptive to the message. Institutional leaders, for example, for whom years of voluntary engagement in internationalisation policies had not paid off in real progress, thought that the pressure of globalisation had to be met by more structural policies and despite resisting strong governmental policies on other issues and defending their institutional autonomy, they were willing to support the reforms of the Bologna Process as a way to move forward.

Institutional leaders and policy-makers felt the need for convergence was pressing as they were being confronted with powerful articulations of globalisation in other fields. The research field for example was rapidly and pervasively globalising, giving way to an international competitive system of scientific publishing and an emerging global market of researchers and scholars. European mobility was on the rise as was global mobility of students, teaching staff, researchers and graduates. The professions graduates were trained for organised themselves increasingly on a transnational level, imposing increasingly authoritative standards on programmes and curricula. The Internet and other technological innovations leading to new delivery modes of teaching and access to hitherto hidden knowledge resources were causing boundaries to disappear and leading to a sense of connectivity and community in higher education. Many felt that structural reforms in education were necessary as well to ensure that it did not disconnect from the other, rapidly globalising parts of the higher education system. In particular, transnational recognition of qualifications was seen as a field where significant progress had still to be achieved.

For the proponents of the Bologna reforms and those in higher education institutions, the fragmented and disclosed nature of European higher education was perceived as responsible for this lack of progress and thus a threat to the future success and competitiveness of the institutions. For example, Europe was perceived as losing to the United States in the competition for internationally mobile students, but increasingly losing out as well to Australia, because Europe's degree structures were incomprehensible and incompatible with the dominant bachelor/master-model prevailing in those countries. Programmes would only be attractive if they were labeled by quality assurance agencies working under internationally agreed standards that would guarantee their international recognition and the transferability of their credentials. Transparency, or its variants of "readability" and "compatibility", was seen as a powerful principle of reform that would advertise the qualities and merits of European higher education to the rest of the world. And for Europe – with the European Commission playing a increasingly important role in the process (see Chapter 2) – this was also a unique opportunity to promote mobility, which was expected to lead in turn to greater European mutual understanding and a new "Europeanisation" of higher education (see Chapter 1).

3.3 Convergence as Similarity

Especially in the early stages of the Bologna Process, between the Bologna and Bergen ministerial meetings, the need for transparency and convergence was translated into a drive to make systems more similar. Convergence of national systems meant that similar structural conditions and regulatory mechanisms should be developed. The degree structures, quality assurance regimes and credit transfer and accumulation arrangements were made more similar by national reforms, while still allowing an innocuous degree of national "sovereignty". This dovetailing was crucial for this phase of the reform process: the European Higher Education Area, comprised of national systems, absolutely needed to make its basic characteristics comparable and compatible.

However, approaching the end of the first decade of the Bologna Process, it seems that the prevalent notion of "convergence as similarity" has moved beyond what was intrinsically necessary. At least, the boundaries of the notion of "convergence as increasing similarity" were not clearly defined. The debate on the impact of the Bologna Process focused on the fruitless question of whether it was leading to the despised notion of "harmonisation" and whether it was compatible with the existing legal frameworks in education (Huisman & Van der Wende 2004; Charlier & Croche 2005; Garben 2008), whereas the really relevant question is whether the "convergence as similarity" approach in itself was conducive to the development of European higher education. This can be demonstrated in a number of domains, at programme, institutional and system levels.

A clear example is that of programmes and curricula. Early on in the Bologna reform process, some reform advocates thought that not only the degree structures, but also curricula and content of programmes were in need of greater transparency, and hence similarity. The transition to the bachelor/master degree system provided an excellent opportunity for the review and renewal of programmes, their contents and learning objectives. In this, making programmes more similar was seen as beneficial for mobility within programmes and between bachelor and master's levels, and for easy credit transfer between institutions. Students should be encouraged to move freely without barriers imposed by institutional or programme specifications, which were sometimes seen as symptoms of academic isolation and stubbornness. This, coinciding with increasing pressure from professional organisations and external regulatory bodies to control what was being taught, but also facilitated by an increasing access to international course materials and resources, led towards the standardisation of curricula.

Comparable approaches can be identified regarding institutions. Critics have charged the Bologna Process with introducing a more market-oriented higher education regime in Europe, with increased competition between institutions and negative consequences for students (for example, Barkholt 2005). This argument cannot be substantiated; on the contrary, in many countries the Bologna Process has led to increasing internal similarities within national higher education systems and, hence, less competition. The creation of national "higher education areas" as the building blocks of the European Higher Education Area has fuelled an inclusive approach as institutions with differing profiles and activities were integrated into a common framework and a common legislation and were invited to view themselves as similar and equal. This was not only the case in countries with an integrated higher education system, but countries with a binary system of higher education also found their differences with other institutions decreasing as a indirect consequence of the Bologna reforms. In binary systems, such as those in the Netherlands and Belgium, the immediate aspirations of the *hogescholen* were to acquire the same status and perceived privileges as universities.

Ministers and other national policy-makers apparently perceived the Bologna Process as an opportunity to streamline the national systems. The reasons for doing so were manifold: to preserve or strengthen the internal cohesion of the system, facilitate student mobility within the country, balance regional interests, safeguard equal access, diminish social or regional disparities in student intake and ensure comparable quality levels across institutions. In some countries, as in the Netherlands, at a certain point a minister would develop a public argument in favour of the "de-institutionalisation" of higher education provision: programmes had to be qualified as "academic" or "professional" regardless of the institution in which they were provided. In Flanders attempts were made – unsuccessfully – to ensure that a bachelor-level students in every institution would have automatic access to master's programmes in their field of study in any other institution in the region. In other countries quality assurance and accreditation systems were used to shift control from institutions to public bodies. Institutional leaders reacted to these developments with an increased, but sometimes dogmatic and hence ineffective, rhetorical appeal for institutional autonomy. However, there were many proponents of institutional similarity from within the institutions who resisted market-like developments which would only favour stronger institutions.

Finally, also at the level of national systems the Bologna Process has resulted in approaches and policies stressing similarities. One of the most powerful messages – almost a "dream" in the politically mobilising sense – was the creation of an integrated European Higher Education Area. No doubt, the prospect of inclusion in an immense transnational integrated higher education system attracted many countries on the periphery of the academic system and even at and over the frontiers of Europe, to apply for membership. Today, the Bologna Process includes 46 countries, many more than the 27 member states of the European Union, and is expanding to the east with every ministerial meeting. Furthermore, it attracts attention from other parts of the world, such as Latin America, Northern Africa and even Asia. Because of its expansion, the Bologna Process had to cultivate a very inclusive mode of operation. This is undoubtedly also a reason for its strength and success. The price for that, however, was the continuation and even strengthening of a politically and diplomatically inclusive approach, whereby every country was an equal participant in the whole enterprise, difficult issues and sensitive questions tended to be avoided and less ambitious objectives, often at the level of the lowest common denominator, took the place of challenging ambitions.

3.4 The Risks of Convergence

On the three levels – programme, institutional and national system level – the "convergence as similarity"-approach has important risks for the quality and, thus, the competitiveness of European higher education.

At programme level, the standardisation of curricula and learning outcomes implies certain risks. Of course, there were and are many arguments in favour of greater transparency and even convergence of curricula and learning outcomes. Academic freedom – still an important value of the higher education system, and consecrated by the Magna Carta of European universities, signed in 1988[1] – should not be an argument for absolute individual sovereignty of academics over programme content and learning outcomes. In many institutions, the control over curricula has shifted towards higher levels of institutional decision-making. Also in more nationally determined systems of curricula control, transparency is often lacking. Credit systems, and ECTS in particular, and the Diploma Supplement (encouraged by the European Council and the Lisbon Recognition Convention[2]) led to increasing transparency and public accessibility and "readability" of curricula. External accountability – to the labour market, the professions and the general public – is another valid argument in favour of convergence of programmes.

The Bologna Process reinforced these developments in its parallel mechanisms and "accompanying measures", by bringing together higher education professionals and experts in intensive processes of information exchange and discussion. The Tuning Project,[3] building on the already existing Thematic Networks promoted by European programmes, was and is the main framework of intra-disciplinary cooperation, leading to mutually agreed sets of benchmarks of programme objectives, curricula, contents and learning outcomes for a number of disciplines. This project and its outcomes clearly are among the less noticed but most meaningful and successful components of the Bologna Process.

Still, the dangers of standardisation and uniformity of programmes and curricula are looming. The Tuning Project often had great difficulties in convincing institutions that standardisation was and is not its objective. And on occasion this sounded like a rather hollow assertion, because some of the affiliates really did aspire to a certain level of uniformity. However, curricular standardisation would be a very bad thing for higher education. Contents and aspired learning outcomes of programmes in higher education institutions are (and should be) closely related to scientific research and hence should be in a constant dynamic of change and innovation. The open nature of science, the complex process of putting established knowledge and theories to the test and, ultimately, of falsification, which defines scientific progress, should be reflected in curricula. The quality of programmes and teaching staff is not only defined by excellent teaching and learning arrangements, but also by the innovativeness and originality of contents and learning outcomes. And probably there are many other dimensions that make higher education programmes, their curricula and their learning outcomes "unique". This uniqueness leads to a certain degree of competitiveness at programme level, whereby excellent programmes and staff attract students and gain reputation among employers and communities. The impact of programme differentiation on student mobility should not be overestimated, but still its contribution to the reputation of programmes and teaching staff is considerable. This is not only true for academic programmes at master or

---

[1] http://www.magna-charta.org/magna.html

[2] http://www.coe.int/t/dg4/highereducation/Recognition/LRC_en.asp

[3] http://tuning.unideusto.org/tuningeu/

doctorate level, but also for professionally oriented programmes. Interaction with industry and the professions can take place in many different ways and programmes should distinguish themselves in the intensiveness and nature of that interaction. And this is reflected in the curriculum and the learning objectives of programmes, in turn affecting their reputation and attractiveness.

At the institutional level, the case for diversity is even stronger. As argued in Chapter 1, the tendency to treat institutions as similar and interchangeable and the corresponding attitude among institutions to copy each other and lay claim to identical characteristics and qualities, has resulted in a number of problematic developments. The most obvious one is "mission overload", the tendency of institutions to avoid difficult choices in profiling and to pretend to do exactly the same things in a comparable manner as their competitors. A recent report by an authoritative group of experts, published by the European Science Foundation, warns against the risks of constantly increasing expectations of higher education institutions and the resulting danger of mission overload if no clear strategic choices are made (European Science Foundation 2008). Also, the recently published review of tertiary education by OECD points to the growing demands put on contemporary higher education institutions and systems, the increasing diversification and the need for more purposeful steering of institutions and national systems (OECD 2008).

Many European universities have avoided differentiation in profile and, consequently, are struggling with a lack of resources to achieve high quality results in all the areas they aspire to and activities they claim to be engaged. This is now increasingly seen as problematic, not only by the institutions but also by policy-makers. The oversupply of programmes for example, often the result of regional demands and the emergence of new institutions in previous decades, is increasingly seen as a waste of public resources and a potential cause of duplication and mediocrity. In most European countries recent policies aim to concentrate research and programme provision in those institutions capable of delivering high-quality output. Competitive selection procedures for research applications and the distribution of research money are now in place in most European countries. Some countries – Germany is the most noteworthy example (see Chapter 2) – have moved to explicit programmes of institutional selection on excellence. For educational activities, however, a more selective approach is still not evident.

Another problematic consequence of the process of increasing institutional homogeneity is the disincentive to innovation. With most institutions pretending to undertake same kind of activities, the return on investing in innovative developments risks being very low. This may be one of the reasons that innovative teaching and learning arrangements, with new delivery modes and innovative technologies, do not seem to be emerging and gaining ground in Europe as successfully as in other parts of the world. An institution engaging in innovative educational activities is immediately followed by another institution claiming equal access to resources and opportunities. The result is that institutions avoid risk-taking policies of investing in developments with uncertain outcomes of which they would not be the only beneficiaries.

More institutional diversity is clearly needed. Institutions have an interest in developing better defined and more focused institutional profiles. Within a basically egalitarian system – one of the strong merits of the European Higher Education Area – there is a lot of room for institutional profiling (see Chapter 4). Institutions should not focus primarily on the institutional territory they cede to their competitors, but at the gains in focus, cost-effectiveness and reputation. Focusing on institutional strengths and leaving behind ambitions and activities which will not be rewarded and which drain resources is a promising outlook for many European institutions. The convergence in the European Higher Education Area offers opportunities for institutions to network and exchange experiences, ideas and resources with institutions sharing the same profile. In previous decades international networks of higher education institutions were established with the purpose of serving the needs of institutions in developing internationalisation policies, such as establishing contacts for European cooperation and mobility programmes. Such networks as, for example the Coimbra Group[4] and Santander Group,[5] are rather large and open groupings. Contemporary networks of institutions serve different needs: they are more oriented towards bringing together institutions with similar profiles, for an exchange of experiences and the promotion of their specific interests. Examples are the League of European Research Universities (LERU)[6] and the European Consortium of Innovative Universities (ECIU).[7]

Still, European higher education institutions are not yet very enthusiastic about profiling themselves. Adopting a better-defined but narrower profile is possibly perceived as a strategy with short-term losses and uncertain longer-term benefits. The basic problem is that the range of possible profiles and institutional identities is often translated into a simple, unidimensional and very normative hierarchy of types. International rankings – and their easy uptake by the press and popular opinion – tend to favour specific types of institutional profiles, which by their very nature offer neither a desirable nor achievable perspective. They operate as ordering mechanisms in the "knowledge status economy" (Marginson 2008). Experts agree that rankings, which have an enormous impact on institutional behaviour, should move towards more plurality and multiplicity, based on more sophisticated sets of indicators (Marginson 2008; Marginson & Van der Wende 2007; Van Vught 2008, see also Chapter 5 of this volume). Basically, the European classification of higher education institutions proposed in the subsequent chapters of this book is an attempt to move in this direction by presenting in a multidimensional way a range of possible institutional profiles for European higher education institutions. It is probably an illusion to expect that institutions would engage in more diversified profiling if there is no politically supported classification which rewards different institutional profiles.

Finally, diversity is also a necessity in national higher education systems. Globalisation produces equally competitive environments for national systems as for institutions. Politicians and policy-makers might be expected to increasingly

---

[4] http://www.coimbra-group.eu/

[5] http://sgroup.be/glowna.html

[6] http://www.leru.org/

[7] http://eciu.web.ua.pt/

shift their attention to the competitive strengths and weaknesses of their own systems and, as a consequence, be less concerned with an inclusive view on the integration of the European Higher Education Area. Certainly, convergence within a common European Higher Education Area produces many benefits, but will have to be balanced by the competitive recognition of specific qualities of the national systems. Within the European Union the Lisbon Strategy is a very powerful policy process – having perhaps more political impact at the moment than the Bologna Process – in which ambitious strategic objectives at European and national level are set and benchmarking is imperative (see Chapter 2). This creates a political environment in which the common European objective ("to become the most competitive economy in the world by 2010") is realised through competitive national policies and mutual benchmarking.

3.5   The Need for Transparency

The basic argument of this chapter is that the Bologna Process should acknowledge the diversification in European higher education and put forward strategic objectives for its second phase (2010–2020) that define convergence not as promoting similarities, but as transparency of diversity within a generally defined common framework.

For many years, recognising the diversification in European higher education has almost been a political statement. During the early years of the Bologna Process, the political drive for convergence – in its "convergence as similarity" approach – for the transition to a common degree structure, for more mobility and for the creation of a European higher education area all contributed to a climate in which differences between programmes, institutions and systems could not be readily acknowledged. However, also the opposite seems to be true: sometimes the increasing diversification of European higher education is used as a slogan. Among others, Scott (1995, 2004) and especially Teichler (2007a, b, 2008) have been criticising the recent research interest in "diversification" and "hierarchy" as an almost ideological undertaking. Teichler (2007a) warns against an exaggerated interest in the vertical, hierarchical dimension of diversification as a consequence of the impact of rankings dominated by research output, and believes this to be motivated by an anti-meritocratic wave in line with the *Zeitgeist* of competition and stratification and contrary to the European configuration of the higher education system. Diversification of higher education is not a neutral issue.

Even if the diversification of European higher education has yet to be satisfactorily analysed with empirical evidence and even if some accounts are rather "distorted", it is impossible to deny the overall tendency of increasing diversity. In previous sections, we have illustrated some trends of increasing diversity at programme, institutional and national-system level. In Chapter 2 of this book the institutional diversity of European higher education – which seems to be the most relevant form – is analysed in more depth. In fact, "mapping higher education institutions" resulting in a kind of classification of higher education institutions is nothing more than a collective decision-making process on what the most relevant dimensions of diversity could and should be (see following chapters).

In previous chapters, the distinction between the "horizontal" and "vertical" dimensions of diversity has been discussed, whereby "vertical" is seen as identical to stratification and "hierarchical" quality. Rankings thus are criticised for attaching an exaggerated importance to the vertical dimension, and not mapping out the many "horizontal" dimensions of institutional diversity (see also Chapter 5). The ranking produced by the German Centre for Higher Education Development (CHE)[8] in turn is, rightly, admired not only for its bottom-up approach, but also for including many different dimensions of perceived "quality", including "horizontal". In fact, the difference between the concepts of "horizontal" and "vertical" diversity is highly questionable. The relationships between the many possible dimensions of institutional diversity are not geometrical. Scott's juxtaposition between "hierarchy" and "diversity" as two different approaches and strategies therefore is not very helpful (Scott 2004). In a given social and political context each dimension of diversity can be loaded with values and preferences and, thus, get "hierarchical" properties. This also implies that deciding on the relevance of a dimension of diversity is never a neutral activity and that a stakeholder approach is called for. Still, some dimensions of institutional diversity seem to have a very obvious relevance.

The argument can be developed with a specific example. An extremely relevant dimension of diversity surely is the academic versus vocational character of programmes and institutions. With the massification of tertiary education and the emergence of the non-university sector, European higher education has been moving from university-dominated and dual models to more integrated binary systems and – as in the UK and Spain – even completely unified (but in fact heavily stratified) systems (Kyvik 2004). In fact, the Bologna Process has reinforced and accelerated this transition, as in Flanders and the Netherlands, for example, by — including the non-university sector in the new degree structure and thus integrating it in the national and international higher education area. Stimulated by the perspective of convergence of the Bologna Process, many voices in professionally and vocationally oriented institutions argued that the difference between academic and vocational was no longer essential. As discussed in the previous chapter, the early stages of the Bologna Process induced a kind of blurring of the boundaries between the academic and vocational forms of higher education. Some promoters even saw Bologna as a way to revitalise the democratic merits of the non-university sector in the context of the knowledge society and to assault the fortress of the traditional elite university. As a result, many university leaders were alarmed by the course being taken by the Bologna Process and there developed – for example in the European University Association (EUA) – a certain feeling of resistance against the perceived disappearance of the research university identity. The result was an increasing self-confidence among research universities, more willing to defend their own interests. The debate over the relevance of this dimension of diversity

[8] http://www.che.de/cms/?getObject=302&getLang=en

thus also becomes a power game between different constituencies of the higher education system.

It would be stupid to deny the relevance of the vocational-academic dimension, but defenders of the non-academic institution do have a point that the binary divide is a far too simple solution to a complicated issue. Many self-proclaimed academic programmes have significant vocational and professional aspects, and often increasingly so. In fact, there is no clear binary divide that can neatly distinguish both types of programmes and institutions; the idea of a continuum better correspond to that complex reality. Every programme and – as a more or less integrated and profiled assembly of programmes – every institution may find itself positioned at a particular point on the continuum, balancing academic or research-oriented elements on the one hand and more vocational and professional elements on the other.

The point is not really that reality is far more complex than the binary division in legal and other regulatory systems; the point is what kind of transparency and transparency-enhancing regulatory systems best resemble and support the diversity of the real world. Basically, at the moment there are two different answers to that question. The first, frequently defended by representatives of the vocational sector, is to forget about the binary divide and allow each programme and institution to identify for itself the most suitable point on the continuum. Each programme then can define the best mix of academic and vocational elements in the curriculum to suit its objectives, student demand and labour market needs. This position has received some support within the Bologna Process. Governments, Bologna advocates and even the European Commission have taken a positive attitude towards the emancipation of the non-university sector and its integration in the European Higher Education Area and the new degree structure and, consequently, have defended an almost blurring of the boundaries. In the Erasmus and Socrates programmes the blurring of the use of the term "university" for any higher education institution was motivated by an inclusive stance towards all institutions. Today, several European governments find themselves manoeuvred into being forced to allow institutions for vocational higher education to label themselves "universities of professional education", albeit for international audiences only. The "convergence as similarity" approach also has had consequences on this point.

There are several problematic aspects to this position, the most obvious the decrease in the amount of information provided to students, employers and society, the decrease in transparency. In fact, this position attempts to avoid the drawbacks of the binary divide – reductionism, but probably mainly the perceived lack of status of non-academic programmes – by completely erasing that information. Better no information than partial information appears to be the rationale. It is hard to deny, however, that the academic/vocational standard of a programme is a dimension that has to be clear to students and employers. But there also is a secondary negative consequence: the blurring of the binary divide encourages programmes and institutions to move towards the perceived most attractive point on the continuum, which will undoubtedly mean a move towards the middle. Depending on the perspective with which this tendency is examined, we will see a reinforced "academic drift" and "vocational drift". The combination of the two tendencies – in my view in fact two different expressions of the same movement – will be a decline in diversity and an impoverishment of the overall programme supply (see also Chapter 1).

The second answer is to stick strictly with the legally defined and regulatory imposed binary divide. This is the defensive position that university leaders often take: they want to protect academic tradition and the needs of research universities. To some extent this is a predominantly political position and not a true representation of what is actually happening within universities. In fact, the increased activity of international professional bodies, growing national and international regulatory pressure in the professional domain and demands from labour markets, reinforced by calls from governments – also made in the context of the Bologna Process – to strengthen the employability of graduates, all contribute to a tendency toward "vocational drift" in research universities. The political attitude of university leaders may be somewhat disconnected from actual developments within many university programmes. Nevertheless, there are good reasons to defend the binary divide. Even if gives a limited picture of a far more complicated reality, by dividing the academic/vocational continuum in two parts, the amount of information is much higher than when the binary divide is left behind and so the level of transparency is higher. The regulatory binary divide also steers institutional behaviour by forcing programmes to be defined as falling on either half of the continuum, programme developers have to counteract the influence of academic or vocational drift. The overall result is a better distribution of the programmes on offer in institutions within a given higher education area.

Yet, the non-university sector argument that this is a reductionist and, in terms of consequences, conservative position still holds. The regulatory imposed binary division of programmes and institutions is to a certain extent reductionist, artificial and, in its consequences, protecting the status quo. It discourages programme developers from risk-taking, decreases the dynamics in the system and discourages innovation. The main problem is that it is a completely input-driven system: programmes are supposed to be academic because they are *a priori* classified as academic. Strong quality assurance and accreditation systems sometimes offer opportunities for *ex post* control, by checking whether the academic level of objectives, curricula and content are guaranteed, and this is very helpful. But there are also many borderline cases in strong quality assurance and accreditation systems in which the ultimate decision – of refusing to award programmes academic status – is not taken. Another issue is that within the academic and vocational categories, there is enormous variation between programmes which is not visible to the outside world. The defensive position referred to favours a clear and visible distinction between categories, but dislikes an equally transparent articulation of variation within the categories.

Some countries have experimented with initiatives that make their classification systems more open. I referred already to the idea of "de-institutionalization" proposed by the Dutch liberal education minister Hermans in 2000, at the inception of the accreditation scheme. His idea was that the academic or vocational nature of programmes would be certified *ex post* by accreditation and not necessarily linked to the nature of the institution (university or *hogeschool*). However, Hermans' initiative was unsuccessful: of the 786 accredited academic master's programmes currently listed on the website of the Dutch-Flemish Accreditation Agency NVAO[9] not one is offered by a non-academic institution. So, the binary divide basically remains a largely institutionally driven system.

The solution seems obvious: we need a system which provides information on the essential dimensions of programme and institutional diversity in higher education, not driven by *ex ante* types of regulatory divisions, but on evidence-based *ex post* documentation. The number of dimensions should be sufficient to allow for a fair assessment of institutions and programmes, but not too many, allowing easy consumption of the information and avoiding information overload. The information should be presented on a continuous scale for each dimension, making transparent the actual variation among programmes and institutions on each dimension. The information should also be accessible, not only in technical terms, but by being categorised along predetermined and standardised formats.

Recent developments make it clear that the need for transparency is paramount. Regulatory systems, legal frameworks and other forms of *ex ante* definitions no longer suffice to produce the amount and level of information in demand in modern societies. Quality assurance and accreditation systems have been successful in improving the information intensiveness of contemporary higher education systems, by providing feedback on essential quality dimensions such as the quality compliance of programmes and institutions. But they too cannot fully satisfy the demand for transparency, since there is no general framework for presenting the information. One cannot expect students, employers, policy-makers or the general public to go through the quality assurance reports of all programmes in order to assess the research-intensiveness of a particular higher education institution, for example.

New developments aimed at enhancing transparency all try to streamline information and make it accessible by handling it in predetermined formats, and – last but not least – to generate information on empirical grounds. A few examples transparency-generating projects and developments can be mentioned, but there certainly are many others (see also the overview and discussion by Marginson 2008). The often disguised but widely used rankings, based on research output, are of course an obvious sign of the need for transparency. Despite evident shortcomings and the loud criticisms voiced against them, they are widely used and referred to. Their existence in itself testifies to the real need for more transparency and the inadequacies of existing transparency-enhancing instruments. They are evidence-based, accessible and extremely easy to use (and misuse). Much has been written already on the shortcomings and pitfalls of rankings. By offering a one-dimensional answer to the need for transparency on the high-status vertical dimension of research excellence, they in fact reduce the perspective on diversity and lead to horizontal homogeneity. Rankings, even if they are here to stay, show that the need for transparency should not be exclusively met by one-dimensional, status-driven tools (see Chapter 5 for further analysis). Other developments try to avoid the pitfalls of rankings and to open up the call for transparency to domains other than research output, mainly the field of teaching and learning.

---

[9] http://www.nvao.net/, website visited on 5 November 2008.

The previously-mentioned Tuning Project certainly can be seen as an evidence-based transparency-enhancing project in the educational field. The project's main outcomes produce accessible information on curricula, programme objectives and intended learning outcomes. With its explicit aim to resist the seduction of curriculum standardisation and its objective to demonstrate diversity and various forms of good practice, the Tuning Project offers an excellent information tool on the diversity of curricular answers to sets of competences. Another recent example is the OECD feasibility study on Assessing Higher Education Learning Outcomes (AHELO).[10] This challenging project investigates the feasibility of an empirical assessment of future learning outcomes in a number of fields. While still in its infant stages, if successful, this project would provide a powerful instrument of transparency in which not only intended but actual learning outcomes can be made visible. This would allow qualitative and quantitative comparisons of higher education institutions on their teaching and learning functions.

3.6   Conclusion

Undoubtedly, the need for transparency of the most relevant dimensions of institutional diversity will lead to still other developments and projects. Paradoxically, the level of system convergence achieved by the Bologna Process creates favourable conditions for the development both of diversity and transparency enhancing initiatives. On a number of dimensions the Bologna Process has created a level playing field, in which the rules of the game are evident. A clear degree system integrated in an overall qualifications framework, arrangements for the international recognition of qualifications, mutually-recognised quality assurance procedures protecting basic quality levels and consumer interests, rules for credit transfer and cross-institutional and international credit accumulation, etc., all this contributes to an environment in which both institutions and students can explore their ambitions more freely than before. Contrary to some expectations, convergence does not necessarily have to lead to increasing institutional homogeneity. The Bologna Process has created favourable conditions for greater institutional diversity.

Higher education institutions now find themselves in the position that the integrated higher education area urges them to find new ways to identify and differentiate themselves and to engage in new forms of competition. The possibilities of relying on national borders (e.g. resisting the recognition of qualifications from another country) or regulatory systems (e.g. inscribing in law distinctions between institutions) to satisfy their interests and to preserve their operational space, become more and more limited. Convergence has created new spaces for competition to which institutions will have to adapt. The previously mentioned institutional strategy, to do the same thing as their competitors, leading to mission overload and lack of resources, will soon prove to be short-sighted.

[10] http://www.oecd.org/document/22/0,3343,en_2649_35961291_40624662_1_1_1_1,00.html

For the moment, two other strategies seem to be emerging. The first is to not really engage in moves towards institutional diversity, but merely to proclaim that one is different than the others. This strategy leads to what Van Vught (2008) has described as the "reputation race": institutions developing various, often sophisticated forms of reputation management, including techniques from the domain of advertisement and marketing. Many European higher education institutions invest far more resources in marketing and other forms of reputation management than a decade ago. The second strategy is to develop new forms of exclusion, sometimes using and misusing information tools which are supposed to enhance transparency. I referred already to some of the university networks, sometimes adopting an exclusionary approach. The (mis)use of rankings to differentiate oneself from other institutions and to define an almost exclusive space for high-ranked institutions is an example of this strategy.

Both strategies do not offer excellent perspectives for the further development of European higher education. The perspective of a European Higher Education Area functioning as a quasi-market on the basis of limited or wrong information is not particularly attractive. The gains of convergence risk being lost if the more integrated system is not working with trustworthy information systems. The mobility which the Bologna Process hopes for will not work properly if students and employers have to rely on few or distorted information sources. The big risk for European higher education is that inter-institutional competition, mobility and cooperation will function on the basis not of merit but of proclaimed and undocumented status differences, creating a European higher education arena organised as a bazaar of undemonstrated reputations.

In order to avoid that risk the convergence on systems level has to be accompanied by the establishment of trustworthy, evidence-based transparency-producing information systems. Proclaimed identities will then have to be demonstrated instead of being managed by marketers. This will not be the final and complete answer to the old problem of asymmetric information in (quasi-)markets, but not developing such transparency-enhancing information systems would entail serious risks. Perhaps the most important risk would be the lack of innovation in the system. If proclaimed reputations can be sustained without being questioned by reliable information, newcomers may find it very hard or even impossible to challenge the established institutions. The established institutions would have no incentive to truly differentiate themselves from competitors. A serious loss in system dynamics and innovation would be the result. This is not a risk somewhere in the future, but in all probability is a reality today. The recent Breughel-group policy report "Why reform Europe's universities" (Breughel 2007) attributes the lack of innovation and top-level quality to limited institutional autonomy and funding arrangements. This is the obvious answer if one takes American universities as the reference point and rankings as the most reliable information source, but in fact the limited levels of evidence-based transparency, the restricted development of genuine institutional diversity and the consequential lack of institutional innovation in the system would be far more powerful explanations.

A perhaps more indirect risk of a convergent higher education system without strong evidence-based transparency, is that this would almost inevitably lead to a situation of "market failure" in the eyes of governments. A well-organised higher education area needs effective regulation and the European higher education system is far from being a "market", but when the advantages of convergence are disappearing because of a lack of transparency in the system, governments may find themselves in a situation in which they have to increase instead of decrease the level of regulation. I believe that institutional autonomy, the hallmark of university leaders, can only be protected against excessive governmental regulation, if institutions engage in real diversification and information systems that provide sufficient transparency to this diversity. Research universities should no longer accept that research money is distributed on the basis of reputation and not on the basis of documented merit. Similarly, both research universities and other higher education institutions should be willing to engage in transparency-increasing activities for other dimensions of institutional quality and diversity.

An evidence-based transparency instrument should be one of the priorities for the next phase of the Bologna Process. The European classification of higher education institutions suggested in this book is an effective and highly attractive tool for the further development of the European Higher Education Area.

References

Barkholt, K. (2005). The Bologna Process and integration theory: Convergence and autonomy. *Higher Education in Europe* 30(1), 23–29.

Breughel. (2007). Why reform Europe's universities. Breughel policy brief 2007/04 (retrieved on 5 November 2008 from: http://www.bruegel.org/Public/Publication_detail.php?ID=1169&publicationID=4618).

Charlier, J.E. & Croche, S. (2005). How European integration is eroding national control over education planning and policy. *European Education* 37(4), 7–21.

European Science Foundation (2008). Higher education looking forward: An agenda for future research (retrieved on 4 November 2008 from: http://www.esf.org/publications.html)

Garben, S. (2008). *The Bologna Process from a European law perspective*. European University Institute Working paper LAW 2008/12 (San Domenico di Fiesole: EUI).

Heinze, T. & Knill, C. (2008). Analysing the differential impact of the Bologna Process: Theoretical considerations on national conditions for international policy convergence. *Higher Education* 56, 493–510.

Huisman, J. & Van der Wende, M. (2004). The EU and Bologna: Are supra- and international initiatives threatening domestic agendas? *European Journal of Education* 39(3), 349–357.

Kyvik, S. (2004). Structural changes in higher education systems in Western Europe. *Higher Education in Europe* 29(3), 393–409.

Marginson, S. (2008). A funny thing happened on the way to the K-economy. The new world order in higher education: Research rankings, outcomes measures and institutional classifications. Unpublished keynote paper for the IMHE General Conference, OECD, Paris, 8–10 September 2008 (retrieved on 4 November 2008 from: http://www.cshe.unimelb.edu.au/people/staff_pages/Marginson/IMHE%208–10%20Sept%202008%20Marginson.pdf)

Marginson, S. & Van der Wende, M. (2007). To rank or to be ranked? The impact of global rankings in higher education. *Journal of Studies in International Education* 11(3), 306–339.

Papatsiba, V. (2006). Making higher education more European through student mobility? Revisiting EU initiatives in the context of the Bologna Process. *Comparative Education* 42(1), 93–111.

Santiago, P., Tremblay, K., Basri, E. & Arnal, E. et al. (Eds.). (2008). *Tertiary education for the knowledge society*, Vol. 2. Paris: OECD.

Scott, P. (1995). *The meanings of mass higher education*. London: Oxford University Press/SRHE.

Scott, P. (2004). Hierarchy or diversity? Dilemmas for 21st-century higher education. Keynote for the CHE Symposium *Weiter entfesseln – den Umbruch gestalten*, 29–30 April 2004 (retrieved on 4 November 2008 from: http://www.che.de/cms/?getObject=250&getLang=de&strAction=programm&PK_Veranstaltungen=53)

Teichler, U. (2007a). The changing patterns of the higher education systems in Europe and the future tasks of higher education research. In: European Science Foundation (Ed.), *Higher education looking forward: Relations between higher education and society* (pp. 79–103). Strasbourg: European Science Foundation.

Teichler, U. (2007b). *Higher education systems: Conceptual frameworks, comparative perspectives, empirical findings*. Rotterdam: Sense.

Teichler, U. (2008). Diversification? Trends and explanations of the shape and size of higher education. *Higher Education* 56, 349–379.

Van Vught, F. (2008). Mission diversity and reputation in higher education. *Higher Education Policy* 21(2), 151–174.

Chapter 4
The European Higher Education Classification: Objectives and Concepts

Jeroen Bartelse and Frans van Vught

4.1 Introduction

The rationale for developing a classification of higher education institutions lies in our pursuit to better understand and use diversity in the European higher education landscape. In the previous chapters, it was pointed out that the principle of diversity is an important basis for the further development of the European higher education and research systems. In this chapter we argue why and how a European classification of higher education institutions will contribute to understanding the various types of institutions, their different missions, characteristics and provisions.

In Section 4.2, we explain the objectives of the classification from the point of view of different stakeholders. Section 4.3 delves into the nature of classifying phenomena. Section 4.4 provides an introduction to the most well-known example of a higher education classification, the Carnegie Classification. In Section 4.5, we point out the design principles underlying our classification of higher education institutions. In Section 4.6, we introduce the main concepts and components of a first version of such a classification and discuss its data needs. In the final section we address the relevant use of the classification as an instrument for "institutional profiling".

4.2 Objectives

As argued in the first chapters of this book, the diversity of European higher education should be seen as one of its major strengths. Generally speaking, the diversity of a higher education system increases as a result of a larger variety in its environmental conditions (in particular governmental policy contexts) and of a larger variety in the norms and values espoused by the institutions in the system. The diversity of European higher education would profit if higher education institutions are enabled to develop and define a variety of missions and profiles. In addition, the diversity of European higher education would increase if Europe's higher education institutions were to be confronted with diverse policy contexts that would be supportive of such a variety of missions.

F. van Vught (ed.), *Mapping the Higher Education Landscape*, Higher Education Dynamics 28,   57

However, in order to allow such an increasing diversity to develop, a tool is needed to describe this diversity. This is what the European classification system tries to provide. The objective of the European classification of higher education institutions is to offer a tool which enables various groups of stakeholders to discover the institutional missions and profiles of the European higher education institutions. The classification is a tool that intends to offer relevant and easily available information on the institutional diversity of the European higher education system. In this sense the classification is an instrument for mapping the European higher education landscape. It is an instrument for mapping the profiles of higher education institutions.

In order to provide relevant information for the mapping of the European higher education landscape we have designed a first version of a classification that intends to cater the needs of different stakeholders – students, industry, policy-makers and higher education institutions alike. For this reason, the building of this classification has been a user-oriented process, involving the various groups of stakeholders from the very start of the process (see also Chapter 6).

Like any analysis, classifications by definition are simplifications of reality. We realise that the major challenge when building a classification is to select and preserve the most "relevant" attributes in such a simplification process. These judgements are of course not value-free. The choices of attributes reflect the interests, needs and positions of those who are involved in creating this tool. Since there is no objective basis for making the choices, we have tried to maximally involve the various stakeholders in the process. A crucial aspect of our work has been to determine the potential or intended users (stakeholders), how they would use the classification, how the classification can best suit their needs, as well as their preferences in terms of which aspects to preserve and which to discard.

Below, we briefly indicate how a classification of higher education institutions may be assumed to contribute to the needs of different stakeholders. These indications are provided by the various groups of stakeholders themselves during a number of discussions and research activities.

- Students
  - Students will be better able to identify their preferred higher education institutions and make better choices regarding their study programmes and labour market perspectives.
- Higher education institutions
  - Higher education institutions will be better able to develop their missions and profiles and to engage more effectively in partnerships, benchmarking and networking.
- Business and industry
  - For business and industry, as well as for other organisations, a classification reveals which types of institutions are of particular interest for them, facilitating easier creation of mutual partnerships and stronger relationships.
- Policy-makers
  - Policy-makers in governmental and other contexts will benefit from a deeper insight into institutional diversity. National, but even more so, European

policies for higher education cannot be based on a "one size fits all" approach. Instead, policies need to be attuned to diversity in such a way that it can be made to work most effectively.

- Researchers and analysts
  - A classification serves as a methodological tool for researchers. Analysts and other experts will be facilitated in their policy analyses, international comparative studies, and institutional benchmarking studies, by more insight into institutional diversity in both a methodological and analytical way.

4.3 Classifications and Typologies

Classifying is an activity inextricably related to the human desire to create order out of chaos. The general purpose of a classification is to increase transparency in complex systems, to grasp the diversity within such systems and – consequently – to improve our understanding of phenomena and systems and to support effective communication. Classifications have proven their usefulness in all areas of human life, even in those areas where the uniqueness of each individual or element of the system is recognised.

Perhaps the classification of animals and plants is most appealing to our imagination. The path-breaking work of Linnaeus formed the basis for a better understanding of the differences and similarities between species of animals and plants. Whereas Linnaeus' work lacked a precise theoretical understanding of the evolutionary mechanisms underpinning the differences and communalities, Mendel's work on heredity added much to a better insight in evolutionary processes. Present-day technologies (focusing on the precise analysis of genetic materials) allow us to fully understand the mapping of animal (including humans!) and plant kingdoms.

"A *classification* is a spatial, temporal, or spatio-temporal segmentation of the world" (Bowker & Star 2000, p. 10). Or, in simpler terms, classifying is "the general process of grouping entities by similarity" (Bailey 1994, p. 4). Classifications intend to assess similarities and differences. In the literature on classifications, a number of related terms are used, sometimes interchangeably, which can lead to confusion. In order to be explicit about the concepts used in this book we provide a short resume of the relevant terms.

A classification should be distinguished from a typology. A *typology* is a conceptual classification. A classification orders empirical cases while a typology addresses conceptual entities. The cells in a typology represent concepts rather than empirical cases. A *taxonomy* is a special case of classification with the main difference being that each cell (taxon) comprises an empirical case. This term is generally used in biological sciences. In this book we offer a classification. We have developed a set of dimensions and criteria to be used to group empirical cases (in our case, higher education institutions) and to characterise similarities and differences between these cases.

In the field of higher education, researchers as well as other stakeholders are attempting to understand higher education systems by developing classifications and typologies of institutions. It is important to clearly distinguish between approaches that result from (more or less clear) conceptual distinctions and those defined on the basis of the actual conditions, behaviour and performances of institutions. The first category (called typologies before) is usually government-driven, prescriptive and often defined by law. The best known example is the binary system that exists in many European countries. The second category (called classifications) consists of approaches that analytically categorise institutions on the basis of empirical similarities and differences. The most well known example is that of the Carnegie Classification in the United States. It is this kind of classification that we are presenting in this volume. In Section 4.4, we take a closer look at the Carnegie classification as it provides important lessons for the development of a European higher education classification.

4.4   The Carnegie Classification of Higher Education Institutions

The Carnegie classification has set the stage in the USA for a continuing debate on the pros and cons of classifications in higher education. The initial objective of the Carnegie Commission, in the early 1970s, was to develop a tool to help (educational) researchers to improve the precision of research on higher education. Given the large differences between US higher education institutions, it proved to be useful to analyse phenomena in fairly homogeneous groups of organisations. In other words, the classification was developed as a sampling device and presented categories of higher education institutions.

Categorising higher education institutions has remained the basic approach of the Carnegie classification. The 1976 edition – the second edition – for instance distinguished five main categories of institutions: doctoral-granting institutions (subdivided in: research universities I, research universities II, doctoral-granting universities I, and doctoral-granting universities II), comprehensive universities and colleges (subdivided in: comprehensive universities and colleges I and comprehensive universities and colleges II), liberal arts colleges (subdivided in: liberal arts colleges I and liberal arts colleges II), 2-year colleges and institutes, and professional schools and other specialised institutions. The qualifications "I" and "II" were merely indicators of size: size of federal financial support, number of Ph.Ds. granted and student enrolment.

Over time the classification underwent several changes, partly technical, partly in the labels used. But although there were differences through time, the backbone of the classification remained similar: institutions were classified on the basis of their research and teaching objectives, the degrees offered, their size and their comprehensiveness.

The Carnegie classification enabled interesting analyses of the internal dynamics in the US higher education system. Boyer (1994) mentions that in the 1994 classification the total number of institutions grew by about 200. About 400 new institutions – compared to the situation in 1987 – are listed and 200 institutions either merged, closed or were no longer eligible for inclusion. In addition to births and deaths, the classification made it possible to look at institutions changing positions. In 1994, some 500 institutions were reclassified (Evangelauf 1994). Noteworthy is the large percentual increase (+25%) in the research university I category. Aldersley (1995) analyses the positions of higher education institutions in the classification of 1976, 1987 and 1994 and concludes that traditional indicators of prestige are still important drivers of institutional direction and decision-making. Higher education institutions apparently look "upward" in the classification and actually try to climb the (perceived) hierarchical ladder of reputation.

This raises the question of whether classifications (hierarchical or not) evoke academic drift between the categories. In this respect it is fair to say that the *use* of the Carnegie classification (e.g., by *US News* to develop rankings) may have a more profound impact on institutional behaviour than the Carnegie classification as such (Lombardi 2000, see also Shedd & Wellman 2001). Additionally, referring to the discussion in Chapter 1 of this volume, it should be pointed out that the phenomenon of academic drift is not an effect of the classifications of higher education systems, but rather presents a basic characteristic of the dynamics of these systems themselves.

The Carnegie classification was again adapted in 2000. Quite a number of institutions (about 640) changed position, 500 institutions were new to the classification and almost 200 disappeared (Basinger 2000). A main difference with the 1994 edition is that the four doctoral institutions categories have been collapsed into two categories. The 2000 version puts less stress on research and more weight to education and service. It also got rid of the roman numerals, to avoid connotations with rankings.

In 2005, the Carnegie classification has been revised comprehensively.[1] The challenge was to reap the benefits of the previous classifications and to inhibit some of the downsides. The new classification attempts to forestall the use as a ranking system and aspires to reveal a range of ways in which colleges and universities resemble or differ from one another. Three major innovations have been introduced (McCormick & Zhao 2005). First, instead of one single classification, the new Carnegie classification uses a set of multiple, parallel classifications, thus allowing different dimensions of the US system of universities and colleges to be addressed. These classifications are organised around three fundamental questions: what is taught, who are the students, what is the setting. The result is a set of six all-inclusive classifications on: (1) undergraduate instructional programme, (2) graduate instructional programme, (3) enrolment profile, (4) undergraduate profile, (5) size and setting, and also (6) an update of the existing original classification. Second, a web-based tool has been developed to enable users to combine (categories of) classification schemes and thus to generate subsets of their interest. Third, elective classifications are being developed. These classifications depend on the voluntary participation of institutions. The elective classifications open up opportunities

---

[1] http://www.carnegiefoundation.org/classifications

to map institutions on characteristics of a special nature. The first elective is on "community engagement" and was introduced in December 2006.

As mentioned before, the original Carnegie classification started out as an analytical tool for researchers. And although it never claimed the objective of becoming the dominant classification for universities and colleges, the higher education research community and the public at large adopted it as the major transparency instrument in US higher education. It is now used by a wide variety of stakeholders and for many more purposes than policy analysis or academic research only. Looking back, the introduction of the classification is now seen as "a great leap forward in describing the diversity of higher education in the United States" and one of the Carnegie Commission's most influential projects (Douglas 2005, p. 37). But as McCormick and Zhao note, "by what is largely an accident of history, the [Carnegie] Foundation became the custodian of a classification system that has been used to describe, characterize, categorize colleges and universities for over 30 years, [...]. The Foundation has taken on a sometimes enviable, sometimes controversial, sometimes uncomfortable role as the arbiter of institutional classification and comparison" (McCormick & Zhao 2005: p. 53). The 2005 version of the Carnegie classification implies a move that in our opinion is the most appropriate way of dealing with this uncomfortable role, that is by radically putting the users central. The introduction of multidimensionality, the web-based tool and the voluntary classifications allow stakeholders to make choices about what classifications, characteristics or combinations of these are most relevant to them. As we pointed out in Section 2, it is precisely this that makes classifications most valuable: to provide a tool which enables various groups of stakeholders to create transparency regarding the institutional missions and profiles of higher education institutions.

4.5 Design Principles

The design process of the European higher education classification will be described in Chapter 6. Here it is important to indicate that the design has been based on an analysis of the design principles that appeared to be of crucial importance in the various US Carnegie classifications over the years. This analysis resulted in a number of design principles that formed the basis upon which the first version of the European classification has been developed. These design principles have been widely discussed with the various stakeholders and were further developed during a process of consultation. The principles resulting from this process are the following:

- The classification is based on empirical data
  - There is a conceptual difference between the often legal arrangements of governments to distinguish different types of higher education institutions (polytechnics, *hogescholen*, *Fachhochschulen*, *Ammattikorkeakoulo*) and efforts to categorise different types of institutions on the basis of the actual conditions, behaviour and performance of these institutions. In the European classification, higher education institutions will be classified on the basis of empirical data rather than on regulation or policy intentions and distinctions.

- The classification is based on a multi-actor and multidimensional perspective
  - As we employ a multi-stakeholders approach, different characteristics are relevant for classifying higher education institutions in Europe. The relevance of the various dimensions of the classification should reflect the views of the various stakeholders. Because of this we pursue a multidimensional classification approach, which allows institutions to be categorised on various dimensions.
- The classification is non-hierarchical
  - Classifications can be constructed hierarchically or non-hierarchically. The concept "hierarchy" has two meanings here. It either can be interpreted in terms of the structure of the classification (tree-like, with general types at the top and branches indicating subtypes; cf. the five kingdoms in nature) or in terms of the outcomes (the emergent classification implies a rank order). In the classification presented here, there is no hierarchy between dimensions, nor between the categories within a dimension. It must however be noted that any attempt to classify elements cannot prevent hierarchy-related interpretations.
- The classification is relevant for all higher education institutions in Europe
  - The classification should be relevant to all higher education institutions in Europe, which means that the classification must be recognisable for and applicable to all institutions. However, we suggest that only accredited and/ or nationally recognised institutions of higher education should be eligible to be incorporated in the classification. This implies that the classification should be related to the European policy on quality assurance, in particular the European Quality Assurance Register in Higher Education (EQAR).
- The classification is descriptive, not prescriptive
  - The classification reflects the factual profile of an institution. It offers a description of the actual situation of an institution on the dimensions and indicators judged to be relevant by the institution itself. It does not judge, nor advise institutions on the basis of this information.
- The classification is based on reliable and verifiable data
  - It is important to decide which types of data are relevant for a classification. Classifications can be based on subjective judgements (of peers, students, etc.) or on more or less objective data. We strive to classify as much as possible on the basis of objective, verifiable and reliable data.
- The classification is parsimonious regarding extra data collection
  - In terms of data gathering, parsimony is important to downsize the costs and efforts of collecting data. The European classification is designed in such a way that extra data gathering needs can be restricted to a minimum.

4.6   The Components of the European Classification

We propose a first version of a classification of higher education institutions which is made up of 14 dimensions and a set of indicators per dimension. A dimension reflects a characteristic of higher education institutions upon which differences and similarities can be mapped. Each dimension highlights a different aspect of the profile of the institutions included. This multidimensional set up of the classification implies that institutions can be grouped and compared in a variety of ways. Indicators provide (quantitative) information and can be used to assess the position of a higher education institution on the dimensions.

How did we develop the dimensions? Our starting point was the principle that the diversity of higher education institutions must be reflected in relevant characteristics, while at the same time respecting parsimony. As pointed out before, the relevance of characteristics depends on the subjective interests of stakeholders. Hence, our approach to selecting dimensions has been heuristic. Through an iterative process long-lists of dimensions were discussed with stakeholders and higher education researchers. Next, we tested the relevance of the dimensions through in depth case studies and both a pilot and a larger survey. For the detailed reports on the case studies and the outcomes of the surveys, we refer to Chapter 6. As a result, we have generated 14 dimensions that provide, on the one hand, ample opportunities for institutions to profile themselves in a variety of ways and, on the other hand, provide different other stakeholders with relevant information on the various higher education institutions in Europe. These dimensions are presented and briefly explained in Table 4.1.

As noted earlier, indicators were selected to allow an assessment of an institution's position on each dimension. The indicators make it possible to differentiate between

Table 4.1 Dimensions

1. Degree level	Information on the degrees offered at institutions
2. Subject mix	The range of subjects offered
3. Orientation of programmes	Reflecting the institution's degree of vocational orientation
4. Involvement in lifelong learning	The institution's commitment to the learning by all age groups
5. Research intensiveness	Revealing an institution's commitment to scientific research
6. Innovation intensiveness	The extent to which an institution is engaged in commercial exploitation of its research
7. International orientation: teaching	Institution's engagement in international collaborations in teaching and learning
8. International orientation: research	Institution's engagement in international research programs
9. Size	Categorising institutions according to their overall size in terms of student enrolment, staff numbers and financial turnover
10. Mode of delivery	The mode of delivery of educational programmes
11. Public/private character	Grouping institutions on the basis of their public/private funding base
12. Legal status	The legal status of a higher education institution
13. Cultural engagement	Institution's commitment to not-for-profit activities in the community or society
14. Regional engagement	Institution's role in its regional context

institutions and to construct different classes per dimension. The indicators were selected after many discussions with stakeholders and various tests in a number of research activities. For more details we refer to Chapter 6. Table 4.2 presents an overview of the indicators per dimension.

The dimensions and indicators presented in Tables 4.1 and 4.2 have been selected after direct communication with representative bodies of the various stakeholders,

Table 4.2 Indicators per dimension

1. Degree level	1a: Highest level of degree on which programmes are offered
	1b: Number of qualifications granted in each type of degree programme
2. Subject mix	2a: Number of subject areas covered by an institution using the UNESCO/ISCED subject areas
3. Orientation of programmes	3a: Number of programmes leading to certified/ regulated professions as a percentage of total number of programmes
	3b: The number of programmes offered that address a particular need of the labor market or of specific professions (as percentage of total programmes)
4. Involvement in lifelong learning	4a: Number of adult learners as a percentage of total number of students by type of degree
5. Research intensiveness	5a: Number of peer reviewed publications per FTE academic staff
	5b: The ISI based citation indicator, normalised per field, also known as the "crown indicator"
6. Innovation intensiveness	6a: Number of start-up firms
	6b: Number of patent applications filed
	6c: Annual licensing income
	6d: Revenues from privately funded research contracts as percentage of total research revenues
7. International orientation: teaching	7a: Number of degree-seeking students who are foreign nationals, as percentage of total enrolment
	7b: Number of incoming students in European exchange programmes, as percentage of total enrolment
	7c: Number of students sent out in European exchange programmes
	7d: International staff members as percentage of total staff
	7e: Number of programmes offered abroad
8. International orientation: research	8a: Financial turnover in European research programmes as percentage of total financial research turnover
9. Size	9a: Number of students enrolled (headcount)
	9b: Number of staff members employed (FTE)
10. Mode of delivery	10a: Percentage of total programmes delivered via distance learning

(continued)

Table 4.2 (continued)

	10b: Number of part-time programmes as percentage of total programmes
	10c: Percentage of students studying part-time
11. Public/private character	11a: Percentage of total revenue derived from (competitive and non-competitive) government funding
	11b: Percentage of income from tuition fees
12. Legal status	12a: Legal status as defined in formal legislation
13. Cultural engagement	13a: Number of official concerts and performances (co)-organised by the institution
	13b: Number of official exhibitions (co)-organised by the institution
14. Regional engagement	14a: Annual turnover in EU structural funds as percentage of total turnover
	14b: Percentage of graduates who remain in the region
	14c: Number of extracurricular courses offered for regional labour market
	14d: Income from local/regional sources

and hopefully reflect their views and ambitions. Nevertheless, the dimensions and indicators are not set in stone. Generally speaking, the classification intends to be flexible, not only in the sense that higher education institutions can "move" on the various dimensions and indicators given their specific developments and performances over time, but also in the sense that these dimensions and indicators themselves can be adapted and expanded. The European classification of higher education institutions is assumed to cater for the needs of the various stakeholders and should allow these needs to have an influence on its compilation and appearance. As a special facility the classification therefore offers a number of web-based classification communities that provide discussion platforms on the dimensions and indicators. In these communities stakeholders can discuss the various elements of the classification and design new and additional indicators, as well as reduce and remove them. For more information see: Chapter 6 and www.u-map.eu.

Furthermore, the classification presented here is a first version. The number of dimensions and indicators is still relatively large and may need to be reduced. The communities mentioned earlier will play a major role in the reduction of the number of dimensions and indicators. A second version of the classification will probably contain a smaller number of dimensions and indicators.

The European higher education classification needs data in order to be usable. In the case of the Carnegie classification in the USA these data are largely available at the level of the federal government. In 1968 the US federal government established the Higher Education General Information Survey (HEGIS). However, this instrument had significant limitations, lumping together a broad range of institutions and hindering careful analyses. Later on HEGIS became IPEDS: the Integrated Postsecondary Education Data System. The IPEDS has a major impact on US higher education. Postsecondary institutions wishing to establish or maintain their eligibility in federal student aid programmes must annually report a wide range of data to the US Department of Education (USDE). USDE collects the data through a series of surveys which together constitute the IPEDS. Most of the data are raw data on students, staff and finances, with some added performance measures. As with any data system, in the IPEDS basic definitions and measures are necessary to collect the data. Examples are definitions of what constitutes a full-time or part-time student, and how to categorise finances by activity area (teaching, research, administration and public service).

In European higher education so far, an overall Europe-wide data system does not exist. The national statistical offices in the various European countries all have their own data systems with more or less elaborate information on their higher education systems. Although these national data systems show interesting overlaps, a Europe-wide data system cannot easily be created on the basis of these national data sets. In addition to the national data systems, a number of European and international surveys exist that offer some information on European higher education institutions. However, these surveys are too fragmented and limited to allow a Europe-wide approach to analysis in the context of a European higher education classification system. As a consequence, in order to be able to use the classification, the data will have to be provided by the higher education institutions themselves. The design principle of parsimony underlines that the extra burden this creates for these institutions should be kept to a minimum.

Recently the European Commission and EUROSTAT have launched an initiative to support the development of a European higher education and research census. If such a census can indeed be developed in the coming years, an important condition to "fill" the European higher education classification with empirical data will be fulfilled. The classification will then offer a wide range of options for analyses and applications.

4.7   Conclusion: Institutional Profiles

Classifications use the principles of ordering and comparison to categorise. Higher education classifications characterise similarities and differences among institutions of higher education. Our European classification of higher education institutions allows categorisations according to the number of dimensions being applied in the classification. As already indicated, the first version of the European classification presented here is a multidimensional instrument, providing a number of categories in which institutions are grouped that show similar "scores" on specific dimensions and indicators. The classification indeed is an instrument for "mapping" the European higher education landscape. The European classification of higher education institutions thus differs from aggregated rankings in that it allows multiple scores for individual institutions. It also differs from rankings in general because it does not intend to create hierarchical comparisons, leading to one "league table". However, this will not stop users from developing their own rankings of tailor-made subsets of institutions within the classification. This is not necessarily a bad thing.

At least the use of subsets of largely similar institutions reduces the diversity within these groups of institutions and consequently implies that these institutions are not unfairly ranked. In this sense, we believe that the European classification of higher education institutions is a relevant and significant prerequisite for better rankings in European higher education. In Chapter 5 this topic is discussed in more detail.

An important objective of developing a multiple classification system is to provide a series of lenses through which we can examine and analyse important similarities and differences among higher education institutions. The European higher education classification offers users and stakeholders a set of varied pictures of the European higher education landscape, capturing in a useful way the true complexity and diversity of European higher education.

The European classification allows users and stakeholders to make deliberate choices about which dimensions are relevant for their purposes. In this sense the classification offers the possibility to present and compare institutional "profiles", descriptive representations of the conditions and performances of higher education institutions on a selected number of dimensions and indicators.

As an illustration in Fig. 4.1 these profiles are presented in a few statistical "spider webs". In these webs different higher education institutions score differently on a number of selected dimensions of the classification, showing in this way their individual authentic profiles.

Institutional profiles, as presented in Fig. 4.1, can be important and useful instruments for higher education institutional management. They can be the basis for internal strategy development, for external benchmarking, for developing inter-institutional cooperation, or simply for effective communication. Institutional profiles capture the relevant characteristics of a higher education institution, particularly because they are the results of the institution's own policies and performances. In this context it may be pointed out that higher education institutions can of course decide on which dimensions of the classification they would like to present themselves. The classification allows higher education institutions to analyse and present themselves according to their own priorities (see Chapters 9 and 10, for example).

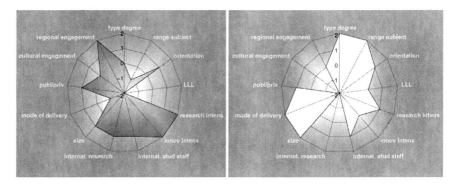

Fig. 4.1 Higher education institutional profiles presented as statistical spider webs

Creating institutional profiles is also a way to address the institutional diversity of European higher education. Based on the European classification of higher education institutions, these profiles can contribute to making this diversity more transparent. They are relevant elements in the process of mapping the European higher education landscape.

References

Aldersley, S.F. (1995). "Upward drift" is alive and well. Research/doctoral model still attractive to institutions. *Change*, September/October, 51–56.

Bailey, K.D. (1994). *Typologies and Taxonomies: An Introduction to Classification Techniques.* Thousand Oaks, CA: Sage.

Basinger, J. (2000). A new way of classifying colleges elates some and perturbs others, *The Chronicle of Higher Education*, 11 August (website archive visited October 2004).

Boyer, E.L. (1994). Foreword. In: Carnegie Foundation for the Advancement of Teaching (Ed.), *A Classification of Institutions of Higher Education* (pp. vii–xvii). Princeton, NJ: CFAT.

Bowker, G.C. & Star, S.L. (2000). *Sorting Things Out: Classifications and Its Consequences.* San Francisco, CA: Jossey-Bass.

Douglas, J.A. (2005). Higher education as a national resource. *Change*, September/October, 31–39.

Evangelauf, J. (1994). A new "Carnegie Classification". *The Chronicle of Higher Education*, 6 April, A17–A25.

Lombardi, J.V. (2000). How classifications can help colleges. *The Chronicle of Higher Education*, 8 September.

McCormick, A.C. & Zhao, C. (2005). Rethinking and reframing the Carnegie Classification. *Change*, September/October, 51–57.

Shedd, J. & Wellman, J. (2001). *Framing the Measures. A Technical Background Paper on Institutional Classification Systems, Data Sets, and Miscellaneous Assessments in Higher Education.* Washington: IHEP.

Chapter 5
Rankings and Classifications:
The Need for a Multidimensional Approach

Marijk van der Wende and Don Westerheijden

5.1 Introduction

This chapter will review the dilemmas, promises and impact of university rankings and their relation to systems for the classification of different types of higher education institutions. It will be argued that rankings only make sense within defined groups of comparable institutions, in other words that classification is a prerequisite for sensible rankings. And that both rankings and classifications should be multidimensional in order to adequately reflect and sustain the diversity within higher education systems and institutions, while making this transparent at the same time. This will be discussed with a special focus on the European context, where the Bologna Process combines trends of convergence and diversity leading to the need for more transparency (see Chapter 3). A particular approach to ranking, developed by CHE,[1] will be presented as a best-practice alternative to many of the shortcomings of conventional rankings. On the basis of cross-border pilot studies its potential for developing into a wider European system will be explored.

5.2 Global Competition, Rankings and Diversity

Globalisation leads to increasing competitive pressures on higher education institutions, in particular related to their position on global university rankings, i.e. the so-called "reputation race" (Van Vught 2008), for which their research performance is almost exclusively the measure. Global rankings suggest that there is in fact only one model that can have global standing: the large comprehensive research university. This has an adverse affect on diversity since academic and mission drift can be expected to intensify as a result. Such one-sided competition also jeopardises the status of activities that universities undertake in other areas, such as undergraduate teaching, innovation, their contribution to regional development, to lifelong learning, etc. and of institutions with different missions and profiles. As a result

---

[1] The German Centre for Higher Education Development (www.che.de).

more vertical stratification rather than horizontal diversification can be expected. In other words, hierarchy rather than diversity will be enhanced, as specialisation and diversification are not generated unless the incentive structure favours this (Marginson & Van der Wende 2007).

5.3   A Closer Look at University Rankings

It is now widely recognised that although rankings are far from problem-free, they seem to be here to stay, and that global rankings[2] in particular have a great impact on policy-makers at all levels in all countries. On the positive side they urge decision-makers to think bigger and set the bar higher, especially in research universities. Yet, major concerns remain related to their methodological underpinnings and to their policy impact on vertical rather than horizontal differentiation of higher education systems (see Chapters 1 and 2). Regardless of the particular methods, most rankings systems share common limitations. The main problems are that most rankings purport to evaluate universities as a whole, negating any internal differentiation, and that the weightings used to construct composite indices covering various aspects of quality or performance may be arbitrary and biased in favour of research, while providing little (or no) guidance on the quality of teaching. Research performance measures tend to be biased towards the natural and medical sciences and the English language, enhancing the stature of comprehensive research universities in major English-speaking countries. These various issues will now be discussed in more detail (see also Van der Wende 2008).

5.4   Limitations and Methodological Issues

Although rankings share broad principles and approaches, they are driven by different purposes and differ considerably in detail related to their methodologies, criteria, reliability and validity (Dill & Soo 2005). They are associated with differing notions of what constitutes university quality, which may be measured by a variety of indicators, depending on the perspective of the ranking's creators. This suggests that there is no commonly accepted, static definition of quality that would fit all institutions, regardless of type and mission, and that a single, objective ranking cannot exist (Van Dyke 2005; Rocki 2005; Brown 2006; Salmi & Saroyan 2006; Usher & Savino 2007).

As higher education institutions have different goals and missions and are internally differentiated, it is invalid to measure and compare them as a unidimensional whole; less to do so as a national system on a holistic basis, let alone across national and regional borders. Unidimensional holistic institutional rankings norm one kind of

---

[2] The most globally influential global rankings are those prepared by the Shanghai Jiao Tong University, first issued in 2003. The second set of global rankings, prepared by The Times Higher, was first published in 2004.

higher education institution with one set of institutional qualities and purposes. It might be argued that the comprehensive research university is the only kind of institution sufficiently widespread throughout the world to underpin a single comparison, and the science disciplines are common to these institutions. There are no cross-national measures of the performance of vocational education systems or institutions equivalent to the ranking measures for research universities. Accepting this situation and proceeding with unidimensional holistic rankings strengthens the perceived authority of the research university at the expense of other types of institutions, other qualities and other purposes. Yet many vocational institutions, such as business schools and schools for performing arts, have international networks and enjoy recognised status and reputation. This shows that there is a basis for overcoming the current situation, as will be argued further in the final sections of this chapter.

Rankings frequently foster holistic judgments about institutions that are not strictly mandated by the data used to compile the rankings and the methods used to standardise and weigh the data. Combining different internal purposes of an institution and the corresponding data using arbitrary weightings is questionable. There is general consensus that this arbitrary and subjective element is a fundamental flaw in the methodology of rankings (Salmi & Saroyan 2006; Usher & Savino 2007). The continual changes in methodology represent another flaw in rankings. Although institutions may not actually change in a significant way, ratings can fluctuate from year to year as rankers change their indicators or change the weighting assigned to different indicators (Salmi & Saroyan 2006; IHEP 2007). Another common problem is that institutions are rank-ordered even when differences in the data are not statistically significant.

Because of the current research ranking bias, the model global university is English-speaking and science-oriented. A major part of the Shanghai ranking[3], for example, is determined by publication and citation performance. This tends to favour those universities particularly strong in the sciences, as the assumption that important scientists publish their findings vigorously in international peer-reviewed journals holds less for engineering, social and behavioral sciences, and even less for the humanities. Also, citation practices differ. In engineering and applied sciences the number of citations per publication is considerably lower than in, for instance, the medical fields (CWTS 2007). Interesting new endeavours in this respect are the 2007 Shanghai rankings by subject field and the new Leiden rankings in which scale (size of the institution), impact (citations per publication) and field are taken into account. It this way a size-independent, field-normalised average impact indicator, the so-called "crown indicator", has been constructed (CWTS 2007).

Nevertheless, such indicators favour universities from English-language nations, because English is the language of research. Recent work on bibliometrical analyses confirms that impact value depends upon whether publications written in languages other than English, particularly French and German, are included or not. Generally the impact of non-English publications is very low (CWTS 2007). Since citation indices heavily rely on publications in English, the facility with which academics

---

[3] See: http://www.arwu.org/ARWU_FIELD.htm

can disseminate research results in English becomes a critical factor in enhancing institutional reputation. This obviously puts institutions from nations whose first language is English in an advantageous position (Salmi & Saroyan 2006). This effect is enhanced further favouring the case of universities from the large US system because Americans mainly cite other Americans and ignore scholarship from other countries more than do academics elsewhere (Altbach 2006).

Despite the fact that the Shanghai ranking does not constitute a holistic comparison of universities, it has been widely interpreted as such. *The Times Higher* gives a more holistic ranking, relying in large part on collecting peer opinions. However, in peer-based analyses major problems are getting a sufficient response rate and achieving adequate coverage of scientists in the relevant social sciences and humanities fields because of the many different schools of thought in these fields (Van Raan 2007).

Another difficulty is that very few rankings focus on teaching and learning as there are, in fact, no widely accepted methods for measuring teaching quality. The Shanghai Jiao Tong group considers it impossible to compare teaching and learning worldwide "owing to the huge differences between universities and the large variety of countries, and because of the technical difficulties inherent in obtaining internationally comparable data" (Liu & Cheng 2005, p. 133). It is even more difficult, it seems, to generate data based on measures of the value added during the educational process (Dill & Soo 2005, p. 503, 505), although data in these areas would be most useful for prospective students. Indicators such as student selectivity and research performance have become proxies for teaching quality. This is highly questionable as higher education research generally finds no necessary connection between the quality of teaching and learning, and the quantity and quality of research (let alone the level of student selectivity) (Dill & Soo 2005). At the same time, the higher regard for research institutions cannot be blamed on the rankings as such, but arises from the academy's own stance toward research and teaching. This suggests the need to carry out the daunting task of developing objective and reliable metrics that can be accepted universally for assessing quality of teaching (Salmi & Saroyan 2006).

Therefore, the OECD's new AHELO project[4] aimed at looking into the feasibility of assessing higher education learning outcomes across institutions on an international comparative basis is of great importance. It is recognised that learning outcomes are an important component of the quality of higher education institutions, however, there exists an obvious gap in its comparative measurement. The question of whether the definition and assessment of learning outcomes can be done across borders is a relatively new one. In Europe the Tuning project[5] presents compelling evidence that the former is possible. But with respect to the latter the question is whether learning outcome assessment can be taken a step further into a truly international and thus diverse higher education context, enabling both assessment and recognition of learning outcomes across the borders of different educational systems, types of institutions, languages and cultures. Another dimension is the

---

[4] See: www.oecd.org/document/22/0,3343,en_2649_35961291_40624662_1_1_1_1,00.html

[5] See: tuning.unideusto.org/tuningeu/

extent to which the use of possible results can be controlled by the sector, i.e. to avoid rankings of the type that stereotype on reputational factors rather than truly inform students and other stakeholders. Provided that the various methodological challenges can be overcome, the data could allow students to make better-informed choices and provide institutions and policy-makers with a greater understanding of their comparative strengths and weaknesses in this area. It would enhance the reputation of institutions that pride themselves on the value they create for their students while at the same time providing the institutions leading in research with the motivation to compete for primacy on the teaching front as well, justifying their claims of Humboltian synergies and leadership in both research and teaching. It may also encourage some bifurcation between the two missions, as alternative routes to institutional primacy. In the longer term, such developments have the potential to transform the sector and its relations with society and economy (Marginson 2008).

From the point of view of students, it is important to see whether or not ranking feeds into improvements in quality and student servicing. Although it can be argued that a league of world-class universities needs to exist as role models, the evidence that strong institutions inspire better performance is so far mainly found in the area of research rather than that of teaching (Sadlac & Liu 2007). In the USA over the years, higher education institutions have learned to target their behavior to max-imise their position on national rankings. This has had disadvantageous effects from a public interest standpoint, for example the manipulation of student entry to maximise student scores and refusal rates, and the growth of merit-based student aid at the expense of needs-based aid (Kirp 2004). Clarke's (2007) findings confirm that access may be threatened by rankings, contributing to the stratification of the US higher education system and, in turn, encouraging such institutional policies as recruiting students who will maintain or enhance their positions in the rank-ings, early admission decisions, merit aid, and tuition discounting. UK research confirmed a strong correlation between ranking position and the relative admission quality of students (Roberts & Thompson 2007). Studies in the US also found a high correlation between a university's league table position and its income per student (Brown 2006), although more so from state funding sources than from tuition (NBER 2007). US and UK research also suggests that only certain prospec-tive students are interested primarily in the prestige ranking of higher education institutions; and interestingly, these students tend to be drawn disproportionately from high-achieving and socially advantaged groups (Dill & Soo 2005, p. 513). Also Clarke (2007) finds that students with higher income and/or high-achieving students are the most likely to use rankings (for an overview of similar findings: Cremonini et al. 2008).

It is unclear whether the extent to which the prestige fostered by rankings is grounded in real differences in quality between higher education institutions, or whether rankings simply recycle and augment existing reputation (Guarino et al. 2005, p. 149), reinforce stereotypes and market stratification (Roberts & Thompson 2007), and favour universities already well-known regardless of merit, degenerating into "popularity contests" (Altbach 2006). Well-known university brands generate "halo effects" (Frank & Cook 1995). Moreover, regardless of the particular selection of qualities measured, any system of holistic national or global rankings tends to function as a reputation-maker that entrenches competition for prestige as a principal aspect of the sector and generates circular reputational effects that tend to reproduce the established hierarchy. Reputational survey data might be an indicator of competitive market position, yet it is invalid to mix these subjective data with objective data such as resources or research outputs. At the same time, a number of observations can be made with respect to the relation between reputation and performance, as reputation is not necessarily the same as past performance. Institutions with an established reputation are remarkably strong in maintaining their position, as this provides them with the cumulative advantage to attract the best people and thus further reinforce their research performance (CWTS 2007; Van Vught 2009). Williams and Van Dyke (2007) find that if reputation within a particular discipline is measured by peer opinion then it is highly correlated with a range of research measures and with an overall measure of performance comprising determinants of international standing. This correlation points to the important role of peer review as the principal procedure of assessing research performance. However, the object to be evaluated should be comparable in size to the usual working environment of the peer. It is questionable whether the individual academics involved in such large-scale surveys can be regarded as knowledgeable experts in every aspect of the evaluated entities, that is, entire universities. It is even more doubtful that they would have detailed knowledge of universities in other countries (Dill & Soo 2005; Berghoff & Federkeil 2006; CWTS 2007) and are aware of all-important recent breakthroughs in specialised fields (Van Raan 2007). It is therefore not surprising that raters have been found to be largely unfamiliar with as many as one third of the programmes they are asked to rate (Brooks 2005).

Finally, it is important to realise both that the scientific journal system has become commercialised and that citation databases too are now completely in the hands of for-profit companies. These trends and facts challenge the potentials of the open source ecology and at the same time create an environment for the open access movement to become more active (Altbach 2008; Marginson 2008). They also challenge the belief that statistics provide accurate judgment of the quality of academic research. In a recent report (even) the International Mathematical Union warns that numbers (related to journal impact factors) are not inherently superior and can be even more subjective than peer review. And also that various groups, such as the scientific disciplines and bibliometric analysts, have vested interests in pushing for citation-based statistics (THE 20-07-2008).

5.5   The Impact of Rankings on Institutional and Governmental Policies

Various studies have investigated the impact of rankings on processes of decision-making and policy formulation in higher education institutions and other bodies such as governmental, funding and quality agencies. Hazelkorn (2007) found that higher education institutions believe that rankings influence reputation, status, stakeholders and policy-makers; that they take ranking results seriously and use them to inform institutional decision-making; and that highly-ranked institutions believe they are or will be rewarded with more funding and prestige in recognition of their position. In other words, institutions act rationally and strategically in effectively becoming what is being measured. The latter issue is reflected in the title of a recent report published by the Higher Education Funding Council for England (HEFCE): "Counting what is measured or measuring what counts?" The HEFCE report confirms that institutions are indeed strongly influenced by rankings; this influence is particularly significant in decision-making, although the institutions may be reluctant to acknowledge this. Rankings are used as performance indicators, strategic targets and drivers for internal change. The study also found that institutions in general find teaching-related indicators (e.g. completion and retention rates, value added, the opinion of students and graduate job prospects) much more important than the rate to which they are reflected by rankings (HEFCE 2008). Latest research from the US confirms trends signalled earlier in that context: influential rankings have led colleges and universities to focus their energies on becoming wealthier, more famous and more exclusive, often at the expense of what matters most – educating their students well (Carey 2008). Institutional leaders themselves are warning that although 57% of institutions may find rankings useful to build reputation and help development, the short-term reputational gains do not counterbalance long-term strategic losses. Negative effects on institutional morale and the fact that rankings push toward conformity with ranking indicators are mentioned in particular (West 2008).

On the governmental side, the weak representation of European higher education in the two global ranking systems coincides with wider concerns over Europe's competitive position as a knowledge economy; compared to that of the USA in particular, but increasingly also with a view to the emerging strengths of Asian countries, in particular China. The European performance in global rankings has prompted policy reflection and action in both EU and national government circles and is often cited in public proposals for greater investment in the European higher education and research area, and proposals for the further concentration of funding in networks and centres of excellence (see Chapter 2). At the EU level, the Lisbon Strategy is the main vehicle for enhancing performance of the higher education sector. At national level, various initiatives are underway to enhance global competitiveness by concentrating resources and providing extra investment. Notable examples are the creation of top universities in Germany, more recent plans in that direction in France, and the mergers of universities and research centres in Denmark. They illustrate the response in Europe to global competition and clearly indicate the important role played by the global rankings of universities. Despite the fact that higher education in Europe does not have the long-standing tradition of league tables as in the USA, and that global rankings were met with some scepticism and critique, politicians in various European countries now set targets for the number of universities that should be listed in the worldwide top 20, 25 or 50. Clearly, there will be strong policy pressure to ensure that the additional investment in higher education and R&D provided as part of the Lisbon Strategy and the various national initiatives will be allocated to successful institutions that have demonstrated their capacity to generate high returns on such investment. This favours the systematic use of rankings and other types of comparison tools as a guide to policy (Marginson & Van der Wende 2007; Van der Wende 2008).

5.6 Alternative Approaches to Ranking: Best Practice from Europe

A better approach to rankings begins from the recognition that all rankings are partial in coverage, and that all rankings are purpose-driven. It is valid to engage in rankings provided they are tailored to specific and transparent purposes (and only interpreted in light of these), and customised to the needs of different stakeholders. Quality in tertiary education implies that education must meet the aspirations of students, the expectations of society, the demands of governments, business and industry, and the standards set by professional associations (Harvey & Green 1993; Salmi & Saroyan 2006). Because "quality is in the eye of the beholder", rankings should be interactive for users. Users should be able to interpret the data on institutional performance using their own choice of criteria. It is necessary to adapt the definition of quality to the interests, learning approaches and circumstances of ever-increasing numbers and types of students – there is no "one size fits all" solution to the purpose of ranking. What each student wants to know is not which university is the best in the world, but which university course is the best for her/him individually. In fact, the real value of "ranking" is not ranking, but matching. As students are primarily interested in choosing a course of study, by definition institutional rankings are only a distant proxy at best and the real need is for programme-level information.

In Europe, the Centre for Higher Education Development (CHE) in Germany has developed an alternative that is better than other ranking systems. The chief strategic virtue of the CHE rankings, one with far-reaching implications for the character of competition in higher education, is that it dispenses with a spurious holistic (overall or summative) rank ordering of higher education institutions, and instead provides a large range of indicator data in specific areas, focusing on single study programmes in individual departments. As CHE states, there is no "one best university" across all areas, and "minimal differences produced by random fluctuations may be misinterpreted as real differences" in holistic rankings systems. The CHE data are presented on a website through an interactive web-enabled database that permits each student to examine and rank their chosen institutions based on their own chosen criteria, that is, to choose their own weighting scheme (CHE 2006). Even within a single subject, the CHE ranking does not calculate an overall value out of single, weighted indicators, as in their view there is neither a theoretical nor an empirical basis to do so. In relation to the students (mainly new entrants) who are the primary target group, the CHE insists that the heterogeneity of their preferences has to be taken into consideration (for instance, whether they are interested in high levels of research activity, intensive teaching, or other themes).

Calculating an overall score would patronise them and would obscure the unique profiles of universities, each with their specific strengths and weaknesses. Hence the CHE ranking is multidimensional by ranking each indicator separately and leaving the decision about their relevance to the user. The CHE ranking does not give individual ranking positions as in statistical terms such a procedure ignores the existence of standard errors. Instead the CHE ranking orders universities per area or theme in three groups: top, bottom and intermediate (Müller-Böling & Federkeil 2007). For reasons of economy, the CHE ranking focuses on selected academic subjects (36) offered by a substantial number of universities and chosen by around 70–80% of the students, which are updated in clusters within a 3-year cycle.

The CHE system is internationally acknowledged as best practice in higher education rankings (Usher & Savino 2007; Van Dyke 2005; Salmi & Saroyan 2006). The system complies with the Berlin Principles on Ranking (UNESCO/IHEP 2006) as developed by the International Ranking Expert Group (IREG) founded by the UNESCO European Centre for Higher Education (UNESCO-CEPES) in Bucharest and the Institute for Higher Education Policy (IHEP) in Washington. In the context of the Bologna Process, CHE decided to internationalise its ranking; besides data on higher education institutions in Germany, it now also includes higher education institutions in Switzerland and Austria. The CHE ranking system seems thus well-positioned to develop into a European-wide system.

5.7 The Dutch–Flemish Pilot with the CHE Ranking

In 2006/2007, a pilot project, funded under the EU's Socrates programme, was conducted with the direct aim to test whether, and how, the CHE approach could be developed beyond the German-language area to higher education institutions in the Netherlands and in the Flemish part of Belgium. The wider aim was to pre-test for suitability as a Europe-wide approach.

The Netherlands and Flanders were chosen as test cases of two different situations. Flanders had no system-wide ranking, while the Netherlands did. The Dutch ranking system is similar in intention and design to the CHE ranking: an information tool for prospective students based on the philosophy that the best match between students' needs and ambitions on the one hand and characteristics ("qualities") of study programmes on the other could be achieved by providing detailed and multidimensional information. The Dutch student information system was established in 1986 with the support of the Dutch Ministry of Education, Culture and Science. In 2006, a web-based version was launched, "Studychoice123" (abbreviated in Dutch to SK123) which had been developed with explicit inspiration from the British Teaching Quality Information (TQI) website.[6] However, with the improvements made over the British model, SK123 evolved into a website[7] looking much

---

[6] Replaced later by www.unistats.com

[7] Also available in English: www.studychoice123.nl

like that of CHE. The pilot in the Netherlands therefore tested (1) to what extent it would be possible to link existing "ranking" systems and (2) the robustness of ranking outcomes by their comparison using both CHE and SK123 methodologies. In Flanders the test was rather how the CHE methodology would be received on "virgin soil" (in more detail: Westerheijden et al. 2008).

In both higher education systems, a maximum of 12–14 study programmes was set to keep the pilot feasible. Programmes were chosen from the areas on the CHE's roster for data collection (which works on a 3-year cycle). Institutional enthusiasm in taking part in the pilot was high, so that all available slots were filled. Institutions were spread across the two countries and included universities as well as universities of applied science (*hogescholen*, i.e. colleges or polytechnics).

For the pilot it was decided not to test all elements of data collection but to focus on the major ones: a web questionnaire on students' experiences and opinions, and a postal questionnaire to gather factual information from the faculties offering the programmes. In the Netherlands, moreover, some consideration was given to the option of making a wholesale link between the Dutch and CHE databases. This proved not to be viable, due to:

- "Blank spots", where indicators on issues such as gender balance were collected in one country but not in the other, or were conceptualised differently in the two countries.
- Indicators were constructed differently in the two countries, as (1) databases derived from national policies and administrative traditions and (2) student questionnaires had been developed independently rather than from a common source and had been administered through different media (telephone interviews in the Netherlands and, until recently, by mail in Germany).

Notwithstanding management enthusiasm, staff and student response rates to the questionnaires was so low that results could not be published, even though many professional rankers are used to working with responses close to — and apparently in some cases much below — the minimum numbers needed for simple statistics. (Publication had not been envisaged in Flanders in any case, to accommodate the sensitivities of the Flemish higher education institutions in their first experience with study programme ranking.)

From a methodological point of view it was interesting, nevertheless, to compare outcomes globally between the CHE student questionnaires and the Dutch questionnaires for the same programmes (administered in the previous 1–3 years, as the SK123 system was based on its own 3-year cycle). On average, overall student satisfaction was 7.5 out of 10, quite an acceptable level for Dutch students (or even Dutch consumers in general) and quite comparable between the two sets of questionnaires. At the same time, this resulted in practically all student opinion indicators ranking "average" to "low" in comparison with the German students' satisfaction with their study programmes.[8] After ruling out technical reasons for this

---

[8] In interpreting this result, it should be borne in mind that the CHE methodology ascribes the category "low" to an indicator in a very conservative way: it is given only if the whole 95% confidence interval for responses in a study programme is lower than the total group's average.

bias, such as different scalings used in the two countries, and convinced through factual indicators that Dutch study programmes were not of lower quality than the German ones, we were left with two possible interpretations:

- Dutch students have higher expectation levels of the services provided and of the teaching support for their learning than their German counterparts.
- Dutch students show a different culture with regard to scales, giving fewer extreme votes than German students do.

These results are remarkable as among practitioners of opinion surveys and market research, Germany and the Netherlands are often seen as quite similar countries. Further study into these possible interpretations is needed; one comparative study into scaling cultures began shortly after the ending of this pilot project.

Several lessons for the future of Europe-wide rankings can be drawn from this pilot project. First, it is not to be expected that existing databases can be combined to yield international databases; data definitions, scales, measurement methods etc. have to be developed on a common basis. As a consequence – our second lesson – it will be unavoidable that an international ranking entails additional work for administrators in higher education institutions or statistics offices who collect data, but also for students who have to fill out an additional questionnaire. Since it appears that "survey fatigue" is becoming a serious threat to response rates, continuous effort is necessary to minimise this, although during the pilot project there were instances where the commitment of management and administrative staff successfully led to good response rates. Our third lesson, then, in this respect, is that cross-national rankings should be based on voluntary participation by higher education institutions.

In a concurrent pilot project, CHE tested the latter assumption: in its first-ever "Excellence Ranking" (www.excellenceranking.org/eusid/EUSID), a homogeneous group of masters programmes in the sciences and mathematics were selected from research-intensive universities across Europe. With a uniform set of measurement instruments a similar methodology was applied as in its "normal" multidimensional ranking of study programmes, although of course the indicators were geared towards master-level programmes and with the interests of internationally mobile, top-level students in mind. In that project too, data collection for some indicators proved difficult, but the student opinion questionnaire apparently worked well (Berghoff et al. 2007).

The contrast between these two pilot projects brings us to a core issue in rankings. As we noticed in the Dutch/Flemish pilot, comparison across institutional types across the three countries would pose problems. While there seems to be an international agreement on the general missions and types of education provided by universities, the "non-university" type institutions were less easily brought into a single comparison. Notwithstanding small cultural distances in general, and a long-standing influence of German higher education types on the Netherlands, the status and mission of German *Fachhochschulen* was somewhat different from those of the Dutch *hogescholen* (similarly in Nickel et al. 2008). The presence of "professors" in German but not in Dutch polytechnics was a small but symbolic difference, signalling different approaches to the character and knowledge sources of study programmes. And the cultural differences between Flanders and the Netherlands were also large enough to make one-to-one comparison difficult too; the discussion on the balance between academic and professional characters of study programmes in this case might be summarised in the question of whether a professional master degree is conceivable, answered in the affirmative in the Netherlands but not in Belgium (similar results were found in Hoger instituut voor de Arbeid & CHEPS 1999). Since the response rate did not allow us to try out cross-national ranking, these potential problems did not come to the surface, but clearly, formal categories cannot be taken at face value for cross-national rankings.

5.8 Rankings, Stratification and Diversity

The fact that most rankings favour the well-established universities, emphasising their research strengths and thus contributing to hierarchy rather than to diversity, has been argued before and particularly in relation to global rankings. The policy impact of global rankings tends to be distinct as global comparisons have been published only in relation to one model of institution, i.e. the comprehensive research-intensive university. This model is the only one sufficiently widespread throughout the world to lend itself to the formation of a unidimensional competition, which, as noted, for the most part is tailored to large, English-speaking universities that are particularly strong in the sciences. Global rankings favour research-intensive universities at the cost of excluding (small) excellent institutions that are primarily undergraduate institutes, such as liberal arts colleges. The extended and intensified competition fostered by global rankings and their echoes at regional and national levels may lead to critical effects and consequences at institutional and system level, unless these effects are modified by policy intervention. Policy measures seem particularly necessary to avoid a situation where some higher education institutions build research strength only through the weakening of others, which would seem to constitute a zero-sum game with no gain in national capacity overall. Recent shifts in Australia's national strategy emphasising the importance of developing a "world-class system" rather than world-class institutions are an interesting example in this respect. Birnbaum (2007) argues that rather than just creating more world-class (research) universities, what is needed also are more world-class technical institutions, world-class community colleges, world-class colleges of agriculture, world-class teaching colleges and world-class regional state universities. This underlines the importance of internal differentiation as a characteristic of a world-class system.

Policy interventions should not be limited to simplistic market-type competition strategies, as increased competition does not necessarily lead to greater responsiveness from higher education institutions to the needs of the knowledge society. Rather than being driven by a competition for social or consumer needs, higher education institutions are driven by a competition for institutional reputation (Van Vught 2006, 2008). As rankings systems reinforce the status of the comprehensive research-intensive university model, there is no reason to assume that competition in itself will generate diversification unless the incentive structure favours this. As argued in the first chapters of this book, without multidimensional incentive structures, "academic drift" in the direction of the single type gaining worldwide reputation will result, leading to more uniform national higher education systems. All universities will then seek to raise their rankings and many are prepared to change priorities in order to achieve this. In Europe, for instance, some polytechnics might seek to alter themselves to fit the new common programme structure securely: the discussion of the academic vs. professional character between Flemish and Dutch polytechnics was a case in point. This draws attention to the importance of policy measures to sustain existing classifications or to develop new ones as required (see below). Policy should strive to correct the adverse effects arising from league tables, and to advance institutional diversity and informed student choice using classifications and customised, multidimensional rankings. At the same time, higher education institutions should be stimulated and enabled to excel in different missions and to develop distinct profiles (see Chapter 4). Therefore more sophisticated indicators for measuring performance in areas other than basic research, such as undergraduate teaching, lifelong learning, knowledge transfer, innovation and regional development need to be developed. In addition to a wider range of indicators, there is the need to develop a good, multidimensional classification of institutions.

5.9 Conclusion

We conclude that in a context in which rankings are "here to stay", care must be exercised to compare similar programmes and similar institutions, as rankings only make sense within well-defined categories of higher education institutions. In other words, classification is a prerequisite for sensible rankings. This goes beyond institutions that are similar in name, to making sure that they are also similar in mission, organisation and programme focus. Classification systems should remain separate from ranking, i.e. making comparisons of "good" or "better" along certain dimensions, judging the quality of research or teaching, for example. Classifications should be multidimensional in order to get a better grip on diversity, and should enable higher education institutions to develop distinct institutional profiles. This view was argued extensively in the previous chapter, which also showed how such a classification could be developed in a European context.

Multidimensional classification should lay the groundwork for multidimensional rankings that stimulate higher education institutions to excel in a variety of domains rather than in one dominant area. Meaningful classifications, reflecting actual differences between higher education institution rather than symbolic ones may assist national authorities to regulate mission drift, helping authorities to continue to shape missions and the division of labour between higher education institutions. Meaningful classifications are also likely to encourage public authorities to sustain a stronger resource approach to non research-intensive institutions than would be otherwise the case. This has particular significance for vocational and occupational institutions. These sectors of higher education would be given a profitable alternative to academic drift. In such an environment, multidimensional rankings may help to make achieving high standards in various aspects of performance not only profitable but also prestigious in the eyes of stakeholders in society, providing an alternative to the current unidimensional reputation race.

References

Altbach, P. (2006). The dilemmas of ranking. *International Higher Education* 42, 2–3.
Altbach, P. (2008). Costs and benefits of open access scholarship. *International Higher Education* 52, 2–3.
Berghoff, S. & Federkeil, G. (2006). *Reputation indicators in university rankings*. Paper presented at the CHER 19th Annual Conference.
Berghoff, S., Brandenburg, U., Carr, D.J., Hachmeister, C.-D. & Müller-Böling, D. (2007). *Identifying the Best: The CHE Ranking of Excellent European Graduate Programmes in the Natural Sciences and Mathematics* (AP99). Gütersloh: CHE-Ranking.
Birnbaum, R. (2007). No world-class university left behind. *International Higher Education* 47, 7–9.
Brooks, R. (2005). Measuring university quality. *The Review of Higher Education* 29, 1–21.
Brown, R. (2006). League tables – do we have to live with them? *Perspective* 10, 33–38.
Carey, K. (2008). College rankings reformed: the case for a new order in higher education. Education Sector Reports.
Clarke, M. (2007). The impact of higher education rankings on student access, choice, and opportunity. In: *College and University Ranking Systems. Global Perspectives and American Challenges*. Washington, DC: Institute for Higher Education Policy.
Cremonini, L., Westerheijden, D.F. & Enders, J. (2008). Disseminating the right information to the right audience: Cultural determinants in the use (and misuse) of rankings. *Higher Education* 55, 373–385.
CWTS. (2007). The Leiden ranking. Retrieved May 3, 2007, from http://www.cwts.nl/cwts/LeidenRankingWebsite.html
Dill, D. & Soo, M. (2005). Academic quality, league tables, and public policy: A cross-national analysis of university rankings. *Higher Education* 49, 495–533.
Frank, R. & Cook, P. (1995). *The Winner-Take-All Society*. New York: Free Press.
Guarino, C., Ridgeway, G., Chun, M. & Buddin, R. (2005). Latent variable analysis: A new approach to university ranking. *Higher Education in Europe* 30, 147–165.
Harvey, L. & Green, D. (1993). Defining quality. *Assessment & Evaluation in Higher Education* 18(1), 9–34.
Hazelkorn, E. (2007). The impact of league tables and ranking systems on higher education decision-making. *Higher Education Management and Policy* 19(2), 87–110.
HEFCE (2008). *Counting what is measured, or measuring what counts? League tables and their impact on higher education institutions in England*. Report to HEFCE by the Centre for Higher Education Research and Information (CHERI), Open University, and Hobsons Research. HEFCE Issues Paper, 2008/14.
Hoger Instituut voor de Arbeid & CHEPS. (1999). *Banen naar en in techniek: Vergelijking van opleidingen en arbeidskansen in techniek in Vlaanderen en Nederland. Rapport voor de ministeries van onderwijs van Vlaanderen en Nederland in het kader van het project Opleidingen en arbeidskansen van ingenieurs*. Leuven & Enschede: Hoger Instituut voor de Arbeid & CHEPS.

Institute for Higher Education Policy (IHEP). (2007). *College and University Ranking Systems. Global Perspectives and American Challenges.* Washington, DC: Institute for Higher Education Policy.

Kirp, D. (2004). *Shakespeare, Einstein and the Bottom-Line: The Marketing of Higher Education.* Cambridge, MA: Harvard University Press.

Liu, N. & Cheng, Y. (2005). The academic ranking of world universities. *Higher Education in Europe* 30, 127–136.

Marginson, S. (2008). *A funny thing happened on the way to the K-economy. The new world order in higher education: Research rankings, outcomes measures and institutional classifications.* Unpublished keynote paper for the IMHE General Conference, Paris, OECD, 8–10 September 2008. See: http://www.cshe.unimelb.edu.au/people/staff_pages/Marginson/IMHE%208–10%20Sept%%202008%20Marginson.pdf

Marginson, S. & Van der Wende, M.C. (2007). *Globalisation and Higher Education.* Education Working Paper No. 8. Paris: OECD. Retrieved August 16, 2008, from http://miranda.source oecd.org/vl=2817342/cl=11/nw=1/rpsv/cgibin/wppdf?file=5l4l3h92jh5g.pdf

Müller-Böling, D. & Federkeil, G. (2007). The CHE-ranking of German, Swiss and Austrian universities. In: J. Sadlac & Lui Nian Cai (Eds.), *The World-class University and Ranking: Aiming Beyond Status* (pp. 189–205). Paris: UNESCO-CEPES.

National Bureau of Economic Research (NBER). (2007). *The Power of Information: How Do US News Rankings Affect the Financial Resources of Public Colleges?* Cambridge, MA: NBER. Retrieved 3 May, 2007, from http://www.nber.org/papers/w12941

Nickel, S., Westerheijden, D. & Zdebel, T. (2008). *Evaluationsbericht CUNE project.* Gütersloh/Enschede: CHE/CHEPS.

Roberts, D. & Thompson, L. (2007). *Reputation management for universities. University league tables and the impact on student recruitment.* Working Paper Series, 2. The Knowledge Partnership.

Rocki, M. (2005). Statistical and mathematical aspects of ranking: Lessons from Poland. *Higher Education in Europe* 30, 173–181.

Sadlac, J. & Liu, L.N. (Eds.). (2007). *The World-class University and Ranking: Aiming Beyond Status.* Paris: UNESCO-CEPES.

Salmi, J. & Saroyan, A. (2006). League tables as policy instruments: Uses and misuses. *Higher Education Management and Policy* 19(2), 24–62.

Times Higher Education. Blind Faith in metrics is "unfounded". Retrieved July 20, 2008, from http://www.timeshighereducation.co.uk/story.asp?storyCode=402533&sectioncode=26

Usher, A. & Savino, M. (2007). A global survey of rankings and league tables. In: *College and University Ranking Systems. Global Perspectives and American Challenges* (pp. 23–35). Washington, DC: Institute for Higher Education Policy.

Van der Wende, M.C. (2008). Rankings and classifications in higher education: A European perspective. In: J. Smart (Ed.), *Higher Education: Handbook of Theory and Research.* Vol. XXIII (pp. 49–73). Dordrecht: Springer.

Van Dyke, N. (2005). Twenty years of university reports cards. *Higher Education in Europe* 30, 103–124.

Van Raan, A.F.J. (2007). Challenges in the ranking of universities. In: J. Sadlak & Lui Nian Cai (Eds.), *The World-class University and Ranking: Aiming Beyond Status* (pp. 87–123). Paris: UNESCO-CEPES.

Van Vught, F.A. (2006). Higher education system dynamics and useful knowledge creation. In: J. Duderstadt & L. Weber (Eds.), *Universities and Business: Partnering for the Knowledge Society* (pp. 63–76). New York: Economica.

Van Vught, F.A. (2008). Mission diversity and reputation in higher education. *Higher Education Policy* 21(2), 151–174.

Van Vught, F.A. (2009). The Europe of knowledge. In: D.D. Dill and F.A. van Vught (Eds.), *National Innovation and the Academic Research Enterprise: Public Policy in International Perspective.* Baltimore, MD: Johns Hopkins University Press.

West, P. (2008). *A Faustian contract? Institutional responses to national and international rankings*. Paper presented to the IMHE General Conference 2008 on The quality, relevance and impact of higher education. Paris, OECD, September 8–10.

Westerheijden, D.F., Federkeil, G., Cremonini, L., Kaiser, F. & Soo, M. (2008). *Excellence goes international: Piloting the CHE ranking of study programmes in Flanders and the Netherlands*. Paper presented at the 21st Annual CHER Conference, Pavia, September 11–13.

Williams, R. & Van Dyke, N. (2007). *Measuring university performance at the discipline/departmental level*. Paper to the Griffith University Symposium on International trends in university rankings and classifications. Griffith University, Brisbane, February 12. Retrieved June 19, 2007, from http://www.griffith.edu.au/conference/university-rankings/

Chapter 6
The European Higher Education Classification: The Design Process

Frans Kaiser and Frans van Vught

6.1 Introduction

In this chapter we focus on the process that has led to the first version of the European classification of higher education institutions. We first describe in general terms the steps and considerations that are the crucial elements of the underlying design process. In the second part we describe the actual process of building the first version of the European classification of higher education institutions and the various research activities performed during that process.

6.2 How to Design a Classification

There is a large literature about designing and design processes. Generally speaking, designing is seen as a goal-oriented activity in which decisions are made in the face of uncertainty with the objective of creating something new (Asimov 1962; Archer 1965; Jones 1980). We have followed a design process in which we intended to create a new instrument which should allow the grouping of empirical entities (in our case, higher education institutions). For this we have deliberately applied a design perspective in which social communication and interaction processes play a crucial role. We see the process of designing as a process of achieving a certain level of consensus among participants with potentially different interests, assuming that such a process requires the participants to explore and discuss their views. We have tried to apply an approach in which a user-oriented perspective is crucial and in which meaning can be constructed through direct interchange with the potential users (Bucciarelli 1994; Oudshoorn & Pinch 2003).

Designing a classification implies developing a set of grouping criteria to order empirical cases (Bailey 1994). Designing a higher education classification is developing a set of dimensions (as we have called the grouping criteria) to group higher education institutions. Analytically speaking five basic steps can be distinguished in the design process of a classification.

The first step is to identify what entities are to be classified and what the classification is for, what purpose it serves. We see the design of a classification as a social and user-oriented process. Since there is no point in building a classification that is not or will not be used, it is crucial to identify the potential or intended users of the classification and what they would use the classification for.

The next step is to identify the relevant and adequate grouping criteria. "The secret to successful classification is the ability to ascertain the key characteristics on which the classification is to be based" (Bailey 1994, p. 2). The choice of the dimensions should allow the users of the classification to group the entities the way they want. The more dimensions selected, the more detailed the entities that can be grouped and described. This has a downside, however, since more dimensions also means less reduction of complexity, which results in a classification that is less manageable. There is no "objective" standard for the optimal number of dimensions, but "no more than seven dimensions" is a rule of thumb that is often used.

The dimensions identified are still abstract concepts that need to be translated into measurable terms. Step 3 identifies and defines the indicators needed to do that. Indicators are quantitative measures that allow the entities to be positioned on the grouping criteria. The choice of indicators is a crucial step as it has an impact on both the validity of the classification and its feasibility. If a classification is built for international comparative use, the definitions used need to be valid in the various national contexts.

Once the indicators are defined, empirical information – data – can be collected. In this fourth step, the reliability and timeliness of the data collected needs to be checked.

The final step is to determine the position of the entities on the dimensions. Based on the empirical information collected in the previous step, the entities are next allocated to the classes or cells of the dimensions. For each dimension, the classes must be identified: cut-off points in the range of indicator scores need to be defined, which requires the development of algorithms to transform the empirical data and the scores on the indicators into a limited number of classes to which the entities can be related

In the user-oriented setting of the project, a sustainable classification needs to meet minimum standards on certain orientations. Three major orientations can be distinguished:

- Creating and enhancing legitimacy
- Creating and enhancing validity and
- Creating and enhancing feasibility

These three major orientations have played a major role in the actual design process.

The design process presented above as a linear, straightforward process, looks rather different in reality. Due to the fact that the three orientations are interrelated, progress in one orientation will evoke new questions in the other orientations, which will lead to an upward spiraling of questions and analyses. Therefore, the simple linear five-step design process presented before is a simplification of the actual design process. In the rest of this chapter we describe the actual design process that resulted in the creation of the first version of the European classification of higher education institutions.

6.3   Designing the European Classification of Higher Education Institutions

The actual design of the European higher education classification took place during three project phases, over a period of 5 years (2005–2009). The first phase consisted of the two basic steps presented before (the identification of the entities and the grouping criteria). The second phase comprised defining the indicators and developing the methods for data collection. The third phase implied a reiteration of the steps relating to the identification of the grouping criteria and the choice of indicators, as well as a process of actual data-collection and an allocation of the entities to the classes of the dimensions.

6.3.1   Phase 1: Breaking the Ground

The first step taken was the identification of potential users of the classification. Based on a literature review and expertise of the project team members, four stakeholder groups were identified: higher education institutions, students, policy-makers, and business and industry. A wide range of organisations expressed interest in the project and contributed to a constructive and fruitful exchange of ideas and views regarding the classification. The needs of the stakeholders were probed further through a process of intensive communication.

The second step was the identification of the grouping criteria that could serve as the dimension of the classification. Because of the diversity of the contributing stakeholders, the wishlist of dimensions became rather lengthy. There was always another characteristic that distinguished a certain type of higher education organisation from its colleague institutions and therefore was considered essential for their profile. In total, almost 30 dimensions were identified. However, this amount was considered hard to handle, which led to the decision to reduce the number of these dimensions. Based on the design principles (see Chapter 4) a draft classification was developed that consisted of 14 dimensions with a set of indicators per dimension. The dimensions and indicators were selected in an interactive process with the stakeholders and experts and were intended to cover the crucial characteristics of higher education institutions in Europe and to allow relevant differentiation between these institutions.

One conclusion of the first phase was that there was clear interest among stakeholders in a classification of higher education institutions in Europe. A long list of needs and wishes was transformed into dimensions that formed the major elements of the base for the further development of the classification.

6.3.2   Phase 2: Testing the Ideas

The overall objectives of the second phase were:

- To test the draft classification developed in phase 1 and adapt it to the realities and needs of the various stakeholders
- To explore and enhance the legitimacy of a European classification of higher education institutions

In this second phase two more steps in the design process were taken: the definition of the indicators and the testing of the various methods for collecting data. Both steps were interrelated, which makes it rather tedious to describe them here in a consecutive way. We have therefore chosen to chronologically describe the activities undertaken in the second phase and relate them to the two steps of the analytical design process.

During the second phase the draft classification was elaborated and tested, including the following activities:

1. An exploratory analysis of the existing (European) data sources in order to determine whether the relevant information for "filling" the classification could be collected from these sources
2. In-depth case studies in order to better understand the needs and expectations of individual higher education institutions regarding the classification
3. A survey of a number of higher education institutions in order to test the relevance, validity and reliability of the elements of the classification and to learn whether the necessary information can be supplied by the institutions.

6.3.2.1   Exploring Existing Sources

In an ideal world, a European classification of higher education institutions would be based on readily available, trustworthy data that are defined and gathered at a European level or are at least comparable at that level. The advantages are obvious: definitions are spelled out, data gathered and checked, consistency of analysis ensured and legitimacy secured. We explored to what extent this ideal situation actually exists. The availability, quality and relevance of the data required for the classification indicators was assessed using a three-step approach:

- Creation of a list of an extensive number of existing data sources.
- Determining whether the data sources were relevant. We used the following criteria:
  - Does the data source comprise information on any of the indicators of the draft classification?

– Is the information presented at the institutional level?
– Does the data source comprise underlying data at the institutional level?
– May the underlying data be used?
– Can the conditions for use (privacy, costs, etc.) be met?
• Assessment of the quality of the data, on the basis of the following criteria:
  – Data must be up to date
  – Consistency through time/reliability
  – Cost of data retrieval

Views and opinions of experts and stakeholders were used to complement the information regarding the most relevant data sources.

The conclusion of the assessment was that international databases are only to a very limited extent available and suitable for building a European classification of higher education institutions. The major bottleneck is that these databases usually comprise system-level data or aggregate data that are not sufficiently institution-specific. Therefore, only a small part of the data needed for the classification can be gathered from national data sources. Most of the data thus has to be collected at the institutional level.

6.3.2.2 Case Studies and Pilot Survey

For the in-depth case studies two levels were distinguished. In two institutions an elaborate on-site investigation took place into the potential strategic benefits of a European classification. In these case studies the very first ideas about dimensions and indicators in the pre-pilot questionnaires and their formulations were explored. In addition to the two in-depth case studies another six higher education institutions were analysed regarding specific issues and aspects of the possible use of the classification. For this analysis a pilot survey was developed and sent to these six institutions as well as to the two in-depth case study institutions.

The case studies provided very positive reactions to the possible use of the classification. All institutions appeared to be convinced that they would be able to work with the classification as a tool for their own strategic management processes. The classification was judged to be a relevant instrument for sharpening an institution's mission and profile. By focusing on the relevant dimensions and indicators of the classification the institutions indicated that they would be able to strengthen their strategic orientation and develop and communicate their profile. In addition the institutions in the case studies indicated that they would be highly interested in identifying and learning from other institutions comparable to them on a number of relevant dimensions and indicators. Developing and expanding partnerships and networks with these colleague institutions and setting up benchmarking processes were seen as important benefits of the classification.

Based on the findings of the case studies and the pilot survey an adapted list of dimensions and indicators of the classification was drafted. This list was the basis for the survey undertaken in the second phase of the project.

6.3.2.3 The Classification Survey

The survey amongst a number of higher education institutions was the major element of the second phase of the research project. This survey served three purposes:

- To assess the relevance of the dimensions selected
- To assess the quality of the indicators selected
- To provide data that will allow further analyses of the dimensions and their clustering and of the indicators and their potential and pitfalls

The survey consisted of two questionnaires: a questionnaire on the dimensions, querying the relevance of the dimensions and the indicators selected, and a questionnaire on the indicators. The latter comprised questions regarding data on the indicators selected as well as an assessment of the indicators.

Two draft questionnaires were developed based on the dimensions and indicators identified and selected at the end of phase I. These draft questionnaires were tested and discussed in the case studies, mentioned before. Based on the results of these tests, the questionnaires were adjusted and placed online for the survey.[1]

The intended sample size for the survey was 100 European higher education institutions. To keep the non-response rate as low as possible, networks of higher education institutions, represented by groups of stakeholders, were asked to introduce the project and identify contact persons. Around 160 higher education institutions were contacted. A second channel through which potential participants to the survey were identified was through an open, web-based procedure. Higher education institutions could register their interest in participating on the project website. Based on the information provided, the project team decided whether an interested institution could participate. In total 16 higher education institutions were selected in this way. A final way to invite participation was through a number of national and international conferences where the project was presented and a call for participation made.

To create the required diversity in the experimental data set, the sample was stratified. The strata in age and size were based on the information on over 3,000 higher education institutions in the database of the International Association of Universities (IAU). For the identification of regions, the United Nations classification of regions was used.[2] In this classification Europe is divided into Eastern, Northern, Southern and Western Europe.

Eventually, 67 responses were received for the indicator questionnaire and 85 for the dimensions questionnaire. In terms of institutional age, the response appeared to be skewed towards younger institutions. Compared to the IAU-based size strata the sample is skewed towards larger higher education institutions. Apparently, larger higher education institutions had greater resources, levels of commitment or opportunities to participate in the survey. The responding higher education institutions

---

[1]For pdf versions of the questionnaires see: www.cheps.org//ceihe_dimension.pdf and www.cheps. org//ceihe_indicators.pdf

[2]http://unstats.un.org/unsd/methods/m49/m49regin.htm#europe

were evenly distributed across the four European regions as distinguished in the UN classification of European regions.

6.3.2.4   Survey Outcomes

The survey addressed the relevance of the dimensions of the classification and the validity and feasibility of the indicators to be used.

The question "this dimension is essential for the profile of our institution" was central for assessing the relevance of the dimensions. The results regarding this question are presented in Fig. 6.1.

For eight of the 14 dimensions more than 80% of the responding higher education institutions agreed on the relevance of the dimension. There was only one dimension (13) which less than 60% of respondents rated as being relevant.

A lack of consensus on the relevance of a dimension is not a disqualifying characteristic. It merely means that the responding higher education institutions differ in their opinion regarding the relevance of this dimension for the profile of their institution.

In order to "score" higher education institutions on the dimensions, 32 indicators were selected. These indicators can be seen as (quantitative) information capable of assessing the positions of higher education institution on the dimensions. In the following text we focus on these indicators.

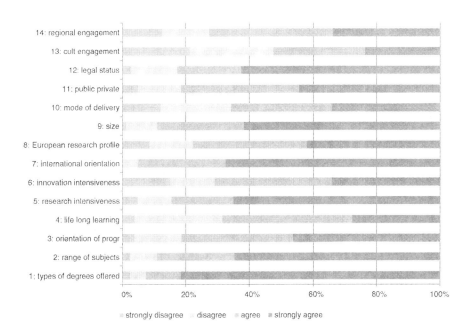

Fig. 6.1   "This dimension is essential for the profile of our institution"

First, we look into the validity of the indicators: do the responding higher education institutions think that the selected indicators measure the phenomena we are investigating? Do the indicators convey a "correct" picture of the dimension?

The focus then shifts to the question of whether the information reported is trustworthy, the perceived reliability of the information reported. Since there are significant differences in the status of the indicators (some are based on widely accepted standard statistics, whereas other have a more experimental character) the project team thought it imperative to check the perceived reliability of the information reported.

The final characteristic of the indicators discussed was whether it is feasible for the responding higher education institutions to collect the required information. This issue was one of the main reasons for the survey. Much of the information underpinning the classification must be provided by individual higher education institutions. Given the growing survey fatigue and administrative burdens faced by higher education institutions, it is crucial to know how higher education institutions perceive the potential burden presented by a classification. Four indications for feasibility are included: time needed to find and report the information, perceived ease of doing so, use of existing sources and percentage of valid responses.

Validity

Validity was assessed in the dimensions questionnaire. The higher education institutions were asked to give their opinion on the statement: "indicator A is a valid indicator for this dimension".

There were five dimensions where the validity of the indicators selected raises some doubts: 3 (orientation of degrees),[3] 4 (involvement in lifelong learning),[4] 6 (intensity of innovation),[5] 13 (cultural engagement),[6] and 14 (regional engagement).[7] These five dimensions have a more experimental status than the other dimensions (Table 6.1).

---

[3]Comments referred to the subjective and "vague" character of indicator b. There were also some comments that the indicators did not differentiate between academic and non-academic or professional institutions. The project team deliberately avoided this traditional dichotomy in the definitions, to break free of these institutionalised labels.

[4]The comments focus on the cut-off point. In some systems other definitions of "mature" students are used (e.g., over 21 years on entry in the UK), which may lead to confusion. It was also mentioned that national differences in age of entry and differences in the organisation of programmes may lead to different age structures of the student body. In those cases the indicator does not identify differences in involvement in lifelong learning but systemic differences.

[5]Comments mainly referred to national differences in patenting practices.

[6]The indicators are considered too "simplistic" and not covering the full width of cultural activities.

[7]Comments revealed some problems regarding the demarcation of the region, and the weak link between the eligibility of the region for structural funds and the regional engagement of a higher education institution. It was further suggested to use the indicator on start-ups (6a) as an indicator for this dimension as well.

Table 6.1 Percentage of responses "strongly disagree" or "disagree" on statement "this is a valid indicator"

Less than 15%	15%–29%	30–50%
1a	1b	3b
2a	3a	4a
7a	5a	6a
7b	5b	6b
7c	8a	6c
7d	10a	6d
9a	10b	7e
9b	10c	13a
	11a	13b
	11b	14a
	12a	14b
		14c

The numbers refer to the numbers of the indicators as listed in Chapter 4, Table 4.2

Reliability

The indicators selected differ in status. Some indicators are already being used in different contexts and build on standard data, whereas others are "experimental" and use information that is not included in the set of commonly reported data. For these indicators it may be that the data provided depend on the person or department reporting the data. To find out whether this reliability problem is perceived to exist, the participating higher education institutions were asked to respond to the statement: "the information is reliable".

The responses are very positive about the reliability of the information provided. For 25 indicators at least five out of six responding higher education institutions reported that they (strongly) agreed with the statement that "the information is reliable". The indicators on which slightly more respondents had some doubts regarding reliability are: 3a and 3b (orientation of degrees), 6d (revenues from private contracts) and 14b and 14c (regional engagement).

Feasibility

To assess the feasibility of the process of collecting and reporting the data we used four indications: the time needed to collect data on the indicator; the score on the "easy to collect" scale; whether the data were collected from an existing source; and the total number of valid cases.

Based on this information an overall rank score was calculated. Calculating an overall rank score is a tricky exercise. There is no clear conceptual basis for weighting the rank scores on the individual feasibility scores. Yet there is an argument to make for weighting the first two indicators stronger than the latter two. The first two are self-reported by the respondents, whereas at least the last indicator is indirectly derived from the sample.

Based on the weighted rank scores[8] we may distinguish three broad categories: indicators with no or only minor feasibility problems, indicators with some feasibility problems, and indicators with significant feasibility problems. To determine the indicators that go into each category, we may either use the list of indicators (sorted by rank score) and make three equally-sized groups, or we may look in this list for relatively large differences in the scores of consecutive indicators. The result of these groupings of overall feasibility scores is presented in Table 6.2 below.

6.3.2.5 Using the Survey Data

The survey provided a rich database that was used to assess the validity and feasibility of the indicators used. In the previous section we discussed the outcomes of this analysis. In this section we present information on two indicators as an illustration of their potential to discriminate between groups of higher education institutions. This discriminating power is an important input for the discussions regarding the reduction and redefinition of dimensions in the third phase of the project (see below).

In Fig. 6.2 the responding higher education institutions are plotted against their size in terms of enrolment (headcount). The figure shows that there are large differences in the size of higher education institutions, even in the small sample we used here. Visual inspection of the graph gives also reason to believe that there is a limited number of "size classes" in the sample. There is one class of "tiny" institutions comprising around 17% of the responding higher education institutions, and three broader classes (small, medium, large) each comprising around 30% of the responding institutions.

The second example refers to the graduate intensity of institutions. Based on the number of degrees conferred, a ratio is calculated with the number of graduate degrees as a percentage of the total number of degrees conferred. The idea

Table 6.2 Grouping of indicators by feasibility score

Method	Feasibility	Indicator
Equal size		
	High	2a, 9a, 1a, 12a, 1b, 11b, 7e, 9b, 6b, 6a, 5
	Medium	10b, 13b, 13a, 10a, 14a, 7a, 6c, 3b, 10c, 11a
	Low	14d, 14c, 3a, 7b, 7c, 7d, 8a, 6d, 14b, 4a
Differences between consecutive scores		
	High	2a, 9a, 1a, 12a, 1b, 11b, 7e, 9b, 6b
	Medium	6a, 5, 10b, 13b, 13a, 10a,14a, 7a, 6c, 3b, 10c, 11a, 14d, 14c, 3a
	Low	7b, 7c, 7d, 8a, 6d, 14b, 4a

---

[8]Weighted rank score: sum of rank scores (rank scores % time and % disagree counted double) divided by four.

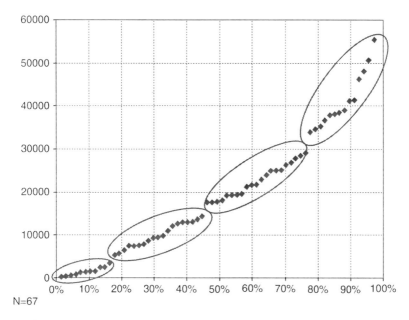

Fig. 6.2 Size (enrolment) by percentage of responding higher education institutions

behind this indicator is that the higher this ratio is, the more graduate-oriented an institution can be assumed to be.

Figure 6.3 shows that there is a small group of institutions that confer undergraduate degrees only, a larger group (around 25% of the responding higher education institutions) that confer mainly undergraduate degrees, a group that has a more or less balanced undergraduate/graduate portfolio and a group that confer mainly graduate degrees. Five percent of the responding higher education institutions confer graduate degrees only.

6.3.2.6   Interim Conclusions

Activities in the second phase informed the project team on a wide range of issues related to classification design. The survey not only provided information on the feasibility of data collection at an institutional level, but also provided a clear focus on the (re)definition of the indicators. The results and the suggestions of the participants led to a new set of indicators that served as an input in the third phase. The survey also highlighted the potential of and problems regarding the validity of the indicators, which contributed to an increase in the legitimacy of the project as a whole. Similarly, the results and analyses of the relevance of the dimensions created a starting point from which the dimensions can be redefined and reduced in number.

One of the reasons behind the survey was to identify the dimensions and indicators which would be useful in the classification. In order to do this, we combined

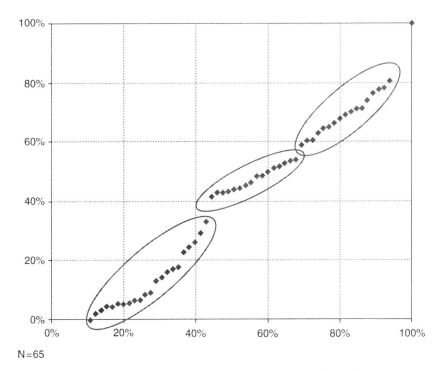

N=65

Fig. 6.3 Graduate intensity by percentage of responding higher education institutions

the information on validity, feasibility and reliability of the indicators selected
for each dimension. We did not use the scores on the perceived relevance of the
dimensions since a high proportion of respondent institutions strongly disagreeing
with the relevance of a dimension is not an indication of the quality of the dimension. Such a lack of consensus is, rather, evidence of the diversity of the missions
and profiles of the higher education institutions. Only if the vast majority of the
responding higher education institutions disagreed with a dimension's relevance
would we reconsider the choice of this dimension. This was not the case for any of
the 14 dimensions.

To identify potential "challenging" dimensions we selected those for which at
least one indicator scored more than 5% "strongly disagree" on the validity and
reliability items and which was in the bottom five of the overall feasibility ranking.
Using these criteria, there are only two such dimensions: 4 (involvement in lifelong
learning) and 6 (innovation intensiveness).

In addition to the analysis of "challenging" dimensions, the second phase
offered a number of general insights that fed into the third phase. A short overview
of the suggestions:

• Include an open question regarding the mission of the institution, preferably
  in the dimensions questionnaire. This will give the institution an opportunity
  to include its aims and, where there is a large discrepancy with its "empirical"

profile, to use this as a starting point for its further strategic development. This information should not be used to classify institutions but presented as additional contextual information.

- The national context should be taken into account. This refers to systemic differences, as well as administrative differences such as the way in which financial statistics are used, or the use of academic versus calendar year.
- Forge links to other institution-based comparative initiatives. For example, there are projects related to student opinions on programmes (such as the German CHE ranking[9]). The suggestion was not to integrate this information into the classification but to present it as relevant background information. Such linkages may increase the usefulness of the classification for students and thus their use of it.
- Create transparent procedures for validation of statistical data and other information provided by the higher education institutions. This is important for the classification (all data need to be collected and presented in a comparable manner) and for the individual institutions (which must be sure that the information provided is presented correctly).

6.3.3   Phase 3: Crafting the Tools

In the third phase, two previous steps, regarding the dimensions and the indicators, were addressed again. The main reason for this was to enhance the validity and feasibility of the indicators. At the end of the second phase it was concluded that the set of indicators could be improved. Redefining existing indicators and adding a few new indicators would enhance the scope of the activities captured with the classification and would therefore also contribute to its legitimacy. It was also concluded that the links between indicators and dimensions were not ideal and that certain indicators could serve to inform more than one dimension. An example of this is the use of "number of extracurricular courses" (an indicator for the dimension "regional engagement"). It was suggested that this could also be used as an indicator for the dimensions "lifelong learning" and "mode of delivery". This observation, added to the accepted practice of limiting the number of dimensions, led to reiteration of step 2: the (re)definition of dimensions. The main criteria for reducing the number of dimensions are the existence of an overlap between dimensions and a dimension not sufficiently distinguishing between higher education institutions.

To redefine the dimensions we use four approaches. First of all, we use the recommendations made during the second phase by members of the various stakeholder groups, higher education institutions participating in the survey and participants at the conferences organised during the project (see previous section).

Secondly, we apply theoretical and conceptual considerations to argue for the clustering of dimensions. While this approach had been taken in the first phase, thinking regarding indicators and dimensions in the field of higher education has

---

[9]http://www.che-ranking.de/cms/?getObject=2&getName=CHE-Ranking&getLang=de

evolved since then. The consultations and surveys brought up new insights that
need to be embedded in broader conceptual frameworks, which is why theoretical
considerations are returned to during the design process at this stage. The third
approach is data-driven. Sixty-seven higher education institutions participated in
the indicator survey. The data provided by these institutions, once validated and
completed, serve as an invaluable basis for statistical analyses focused on the
redefinition and reduction of the number of dimensions. Finally, we use interest
groups (or classification communities) to inform our decisions regarding the redefinition and reduction of dimensions. The creation of classification communities was
suggested during a project conference and emerged as a main result of the second
phase of the European classification research project. It was recommended that the
project team set up communities of institutions willing to invest in developing a
more comprehensive set of indicators for classifying higher education institutions
in specific dimensions and aspects (see Box 6.1). Such a community of interested
institutions could play an active role in developing indicators and could advise the
project team on dimensions and underlying indicators. Participation would be on a
voluntary basis. Working with such a community could enhance the validity, feasibility and legitimacy of the indicators and dimensions used.

Box 6.1 Classification communities

Involvement in lifelong learning

*Current indicator: 4a: number of adult learners as a percentage of total
number of students by type of degree*

Although most stakeholders claimed that this dimension was very relevant,
there was no consensus on how to capture the dimension. The results on the
indicator chosen were rather surprising, as for many responding institutions it
proved to be time-consuming to provide the data in the format required. It was
concluded that this dimension should be reviewed and possibly integrated
with another (e.g. mode of delivery).

Innovation intensiveness

*Current indicators: 6a (number of start-ups); 6b (number of patent applica-
tions filed); 6c (annual licensing income); 6d (revenues from privately funded
research contracts as a percentage of total research revenues).*

There were comments on the narrow focus of the indicators for this dimension.
It was suggested that some indicators should be included signalling innovation in teaching, curricula and research, as well as for innovation in the arts.

International orientation teaching and staff

*Current indicators: 7a (number of degree-seeking students with foreign
nationality as percentage of total enrolment); 7b (number of incoming
students in European exchange programmes as percentage of total enrolment);*

Box 6.1 (continued)

7c (number of students sent abroad in European exchange programmes); 7d (international staff members as percentage of total staff); 7e (number of programmes offered abroad).

It was suggested that "nationality of qualifying diploma" should be used (where the diploma of secondary education was awarded) instead of "nationality of student" to distinguish between national and international students. It was recommended that the project team set up a community of institutions willing to invest in developing a more comprehensive set of indicators for this dimension.

Cultural engagement

Current indicators: 13a (number of official concerts and performances (co)-organised by the institution); 13b (number of official exhibitions (co)-organised by the institution).

The main reason for retaining the dimension "cultural engagement" and investing in the development of better indicators for this is its relevance for particular groups of institutions. Several groups of institutions (arts and music schools) have already expressed their willingness to join a community in this area.

Regional engagement

Current indicators:14a (annual turnover in EU structural funds as percentage of total turnover); 14b (number of graduates remaining in the region as percentage of total graduates); 14c (number of extracurricular courses offered for regional labour market); 14d (importance of local/regional income sources).

It was recommended that the project team set up a community of institutions willing to invest in developing better indicators for regional engagement, and that the indicator "number of extracurricular courses" be used for both dimensions "lifelong learning" and "mode of delivery". It was also suggested that the number of partnerships with business and industry be included as an indicator in measuring "regional engagement".

Business engagement (new)

One potential use of the classification is in facilitating business-university cooperation. At the Berlin conference it was noted that the current set of dimensions and indicators do not adequately reflect activity levels in this field. It was therefore suggested to include a dimension entitled "employer engagement" which would cover not only business-university cooperation but also issues such as human resource management and career perspectives. Since this dimension was not on the original list, a community will be created to kick off the debate and possible creation of this new dimension and its underlying indicators.

In addition to redefining the dimensions and indicators, a further process of data collection is organised in phase 3 of the project. The data provided by the higher education institution in the classification survey needed to be completed and validated. The first dataset was only the starting point for the development of the classification tool. The intention is to let this core grow, as higher education institutions that did not participate in the survey now have the opportunity to submit their data through a renewed online questionnaire. This continuous data collection process will first feed into the further development of the classification tool and later on, hopefully, into the implementation of the classification. Thus far, only a first version of the European higher education classification has been presented. In the coming years the continuing data collection process and the results from the classification communities will lead to one or more further versions.

The final step is to allocate the participating higher education institutions to the various "cells" of the multidimensional classification space. The position of an individual higher education institution on each dimension is based on its "scores" on the underlying indicators and the algorithm through which those scores are combined into a position on the dimension. However, this technical positioning is only part of the story of this methodological design step. As important is an effective and responsible way of communicating these positions. The various stakeholders need to be involved in this process and attractive, simple and flexible communication instruments need to be designed. This is certainly a challenge for the further development of the classification tool.

6.4 Conclusion

In this chapter we reported on the actual design process of the European higher education classification so far. We presented the various design steps and the results of the research activities that were undertaken to inform these steps. The overall result is the first version of the classification as presented in Chapter 4 of this book. This first version is based on extensive communication with stakeholders and several analyses regarding the relevance of the dimensions of the classification and the validity and feasibility of the indicators.

Our overall conclusion is that it is certainly possible to design a multidimensional European classification of higher education institutions and to use such a classification in the contexts of institutional strategies and system-level policies. A European higher education classification is an interesting and effective instrument to make the diversity of European higher education transparent and to offer opportunities to make use of such an increased transparency. It should also be noted, however, that designing a classification is a more or less continuous process. As indicated in Chapter 4, the classification should be flexible not only in the sense that the higher education institutions can change their positions on the dimensions over time, but also in the sense that the dimensions and indicators themselves can be adapted and expanded. The classification communities discussed in this chapter are a user-oriented instrument for this. In addition, the first phase of the data collection process regarding the indicators has shown that valuable insights can arise from further data-gathering. In years to come a solid database will hopefully be developed, allowing both a relevant positioning of higher education institutions on the various dimensions of the classification and a further refinement of the classification instrument itself.

References

Asimov, M. (1962). *Introduction to Design*. Englewood Cliffs, NJ: Prentice Hall.
Archer, B.L. (1965). *Systemic Method for Designers*. London: Council of Industrial Design.
Bailey, K.D. (1994). *Typologies and Taxonomies, An Introduction to Classification Techniques*. Thousands Oaks, CA: Sage.
Bucciarelli, L.L. (1994). *Designing Engineers*. Cambridge, MA: MIT Press.
Jones, J.C. (1980). *Design Methods*. New York: Wiley.
Oudshoorn, N. & Pinch, T. (Eds.). (2003). *How Users Matter, the Co-construction of Users and Technology*. Cambridge, MA: MIT Press.

Chapter 7
Using the Classification in the European Higher Education Area

Sybille Reichert

7.1 Introduction

In this chapter the focus will be on the potential use of the European classification of higher education institutions in the European Higher Education Area (EHEA). This chapter will explore the challenges both national and European higher education systems are facing in terms of institutional diversity. The basic characteristics of the European Higher Education Area will be explored and analysed and in particular the contribution the European higher education classification can make to this area will be explored. What exactly can the classification contribute to the EHEA, to its diversification or convergence, and in which respects will it help to increase transparency of higher education in Europe?

7.2 Institutional Diversity: A Challenge for the Intertwined European Higher Education Landscape

With rising participation rates and an increasingly wide range of stakeholder demands, European higher education institutions find themselves under rising pressures to diversify their provision. As discussed in Chapter 2, more and more national policy-makers join the choir of those calling for institutional diversity. Such calls can be heard clearly in the UK, for example, where the issue of diversity is the red thread that runs through the most recent White Paper "The Future of Higher Education" (Department for Education and Skills 2003). Combining aims of enhanced research excellence and innovation performance with an agenda of widening participation, the UK White Paper may well be a call for a diversity policy for higher education. In France, long-standing institutional traditions and existing institutional boundaries are being reviewed and revised against the background of diversified needs and international competition. Universities and other higher education institutions, including the formerly secluded *Grandes Ecoles*, are urged to join forces as institutions with complementary profiles in common regional PRES (*Pôle de Recherche et d'Enseignement Supérieur*) and the "Campus" initiative prioritises 10 university clus-

F. van Vught (ed.), *Mapping the Higher Education Landscape*, Higher Education Dynamics 28, 105
© Springer Science+Business Media B.V. 2009

ters for substantial research infrastructure support. At the same time, individual types of institutions are being redefined or critically reviewed. Even the established elite flagships, the *Grandes Ecoles*, are being asked to rethink their institutional definitions in light of broadened missions and student clienteles (Veltz 2007). In Germany, the *Exzellenzinitiative* has dispelled the former egalitarian myth of all German universities being equal in quality by selecting the nine highest-performing and strategically-oriented universities for privileged support. In Norway, the question of diversity has been the key focus of a national Higher Education Commission (Stjernø Commission 2008) which has proposed sweeping reforms to address the issue, focussing on two scenarios, a less likely regional model and a more probable differentiation model. The regional model would focus on geography as the basis for mergers of colleges and universities into one (including a reduction of the number of institutions from 38 to 10 larger institutions) while the differentiation model would develop strict guidelines for university classification. These are just a few examples of national systems trying to reshape their higher education landscapes and to redefine institutional profiles. In an age of wider demands and global competition, institutional diversity has become one of the key issues of European higher education policies.

But while there seems to be a growing consensus that institutional diversity is a value to be promoted (Douglas 2004; Guri-Rosenblit et al. 2007; see also Chapter 1 for an inventory of arguments), there is hardly any agreement as to the aspects or degrees of diversity which should be prioritised and at which levels in the system. In different systems, the values of diversity vary between and within institutions, as do the degrees of diversity deemed desirable. At an even more basic level, neither institutional leaders nor system level actors would be in a position to judge how diverse their institutions actually are with respect to different dimensions of higher education. Accordingly, policy-makers would hardly be in a position to measure their own success since the degrees of diversity which exist within their systems are almost unknown, in any regard.

The research literature on institutional diversity, discussed in the first chapters of this book, to a large extent consists of theoretical interpretations of the conditions and drivers of diversification or convergence or of historical accounts of recent developments in national higher education systems. As Huisman et al. (2007) observe "there are many opinions (partial) views, sketchy evaluations of the level of diversity" but "hardly any clear-cut empirical evidence of how and why diversity evolves through time and differs between countries". The empirical studies that have been conducted (and are discussed in Chapter 1 of this volume) must rely on a limited set of indicators due to lack of data at institutional level. For international studies, systematic empirical research is even more constrained given the lack of transnationally comparable data. Hence the few longitudinal studies which trace higher education developments between several countries to ascertain whether diversification or convergence have occurred are limited in their choice of indicators. To make a wider range of internationally comparable data available is thus urgently needed as it would enable researchers, observers and policy-makers to make informed, reliable judgements about the diversity of higher education structures and their developments.

The above-described problems become even more pressing in an increasingly intertwined higher education landscape such as the European Higher Education Area (EHEA). While European policy-makers have entered a common process of policy development and seek to extend the mutual readability of each others' systems, they are still challenged by the lack of reliable and comparable data on basic features of institutional provision that could make their systems readable across borders. Thus, the key action lines of the Bologna Process are either aimed at or linked to attempts to increase transparency across national boundaries, across and beyond Europe. The concern of the European higher education classification with transparency of the multiple dimensions of higher education is close in spirit to the transparency agenda of the Bologna Process (see Chapter 3 of this book). As may have been expected, the policy issue of institutional diversity has not only become prominent in individual national higher education debates in Europe, but has also now entered the horizon of the European Bologna Process, as recent Bologna-related conferences confirm (Ghent Bologna seminar 2008, EAIE plenary on The Future of Bologna 2008). In this context, European policy-makers find themselves in a particularly challenging position. On the one hand, they pursue the common aims of creating an intertwined, structurally convergent higher education landscape, the European Higher Education Area. On the other, they would like to ensure and even celebrate the diversity of such a European Higher Education Area.

7.3   The European Higher Education Area

Let us first clarify what is meant by the term "European Higher Education Area." It is commonly associated with the Bologna reform goals and the process accompanying their realisation. While the interpretations of what this means for different national policy discourses may vary greatly, two ingredients are common to all:

1. The vision of a common European Higher Education Area imagines students and academics choosing freely and flexibly where they want to study, teach and conduct research, on the basis of trustworthy information and with the assurance that their performance will be recognised in other parts of Europe. To allow for such free movement and recognition across national boundaries, governments and higher education representative organisations are developing an array of instruments designed to render the structures, aims and even quality of higher education provision more transparent. Moreover, degree structures and quality assurance methods are being made compatible enough to allow for judgements in one system to be "readable" through the eyes of another and thus even transferable if the information reveals comparable profiles and quality standards.
2. For most European and national policy-makers and some higher education leaders the vision of a European Higher Education Area is also associated with a response to growing global competition. In this logic, transparency of structures and quality labels would only be the first step towards revealing room

for improvements, improving efficiency, effectiveness and quality (for most European education ministers, preferably without increasing investment significantly), so as to compete more successfully in attracting students, teachers and researchers from other countries inside or outside of Europe.

Beyond the European and national discourses related to the Bologna aims proper, the European Higher Education Area may also be understood as an interesting new form and environment of policy development in which national policy-makers agree voluntarily to adapt each others' approaches to a common set of goals within a process which is governed by "soft norms". European ministers and associated policy-makers have thus created a highly interrelated group of national systems which are increasingly osmotic and interdependent in their understanding and approaches to key issues of higher education policy. European and different national policy debates and solutions influence each other with shorter and shorter lag times. This could lead to more or less welcome convergence between these systems. Both successes and mistakes are more easily imitated than before. Associated with such dense interrelatedness is the question of whether and how institutions and systems can position themselves more advantageously in this common landscape. However, without reliable data, neither policy-makers nor institutional leaders would be able to ascertain their relative position in this changing landscape. Only with respect to the few Bologna action lines would there be some comparable data to reveal whether convergence has occurred. Otherwise, they could not tell in which respects their policy approaches and explicit or implicit incentives have made their systems or institutions diverge or converge.

What, then, can the classification presented in this book contribute to such an emerging European Higher Education Area and its discontents? First and foremost, it carries the logic of improved transparency and trustworthiness of transnational information flows one step further. So far, the Bologna reforms have focused on transparency by producing more readable degree structures (compatible bachelors and masters and a common transcript, the Diploma Supplement), more transferable parts of courses in the common currency of credits (ECTS), and more compatible Quality Assurance methodologies, standards and guidelines (through the European QA Standards and Guidelines), all of which have concerned and preoccupied higher education institutions. The European higher education classification now attempts to increase transparency further by extending it to the whole gamut of institutional activities and the resulting institutional profiles. At heart, the classification seeks to render the diversity of higher education in Europe as transparent as an indicator-based approach could possibly make it.

The European classification of higher education institutions may thus provide strategically relevant comparative data on institutional performance, at least in so far as scope and level of activity are concerned, to help realistic advantageous institutional profiling. But the information it provides not only helps institutional leaders. It may also help policy-makers to become more aware of major systemic shifts in the higher education landscapes with which they are concerned, including comparisons between different higher education systems.

7.4 Potential Use of the European Higher Education Classification

Hence the European higher education classification offers a range of new opportunities to prepare informed choices for individuals, institutions and national higher education policy-makers.

For individuals, the classification can provide a quick first insight into the level of activity of a given institution in a particular dimension of its provision. Such opportunities may be of interest to a whole range of different individuals, such as students, teachers, doctoral candidates, researchers, institutional leaders, administrators or company representatives interested in partnerships with higher education institutions. Students or researchers wanting to know more about a given institution can find out about the relative distribution between undergraduate or graduate provision, the distribution of programmes over subjects or types of orientation (professional or academic), the volume of activity related to lifelong learning or distance learning, the level of research production and income, the volume of relations with industry or the degree of attention to regional partnerships and continuing education. While these insights will not say much about the individual context a particular researcher or student is interested in, they will provide a picture of the volume of activity and some of the priorities established over time by a certain institution. Even if some definitions may not be exact, such as where the boundaries lie between "professional" of "academic" programmes, the overall map of the institution will still differ in enlightening ways from other institutions so that some suggestion or at least a hypothesis of the institutional character may emerge.

To illustrate the point, one may apply individual examples to the contribution which could be offered by the data reported in Chapter 6. It should be noted that this data (from the classification project survey) cannot be considered representative since it relies on test samples which constitute only a small (though well-distributed) sample of the European Higher Education Area. But it is still useful to illustrate how the sort of the data which the classification will make available when it is fully established will help to inform higher education users in Europe.

As a first example, one may take the prospective doctoral student interested in deciding on his or her next destination for study and research. Of course, prospective doctoral candidates will make their choices based mainly on the reputation of the doctoral supervisors and their research record, and on their impression of the doctoral programme. But they will also be interested to find out what opportunities may be on offer from the institutional environment in which they will work. Here, classification survey data, as provided in the first test samples in the project report (CHEPS 2008) can be of help. The doctoral candidate, for example, may be interested in comparing how strongly the institution is focussed on doctoral education in the first place, since such a focus is likely to result in a wider range of support services and will imply a highly vested interest of the institution's management in the quality of its doctoral provision, and the latter strongly contributes to the institution's profile. Comparing the "doctoral intensity" of different institutions will

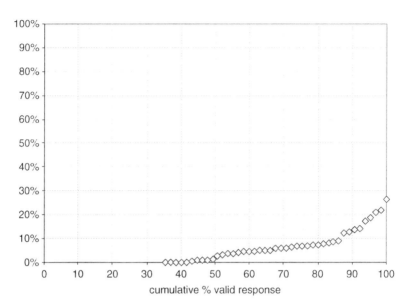

Fig. 7.1 Doctorate degrees awarded as percentage of total number of degrees awarded

give a rather varied picture in Europe, as the test sample of the 67 widely spread institutions shows (Fig. 7.1). Beyond the 35% of institutions which have no doctoral degrees, the vast majority of institutions have less than 10% doctoral degrees in their overall degree structure. While the prospective doctoral student will presumably still choose the future institution on the basis of the quality of its doctoral programme or of an individual research group or scholar as supervisor, he or she may want to check in greater detail whether the institutional support for doctoral students is sufficient for his or her purposes.

Another data set of interest to a prospective doctoral candidate is the number of peer-reviewed publications per academic staff member (Fig. 7.2), since it reflects the overall level of international research intensity at the institution, compared to other institutions in Europe. This may be of relevance if the student is strongly interested in seeking stimulation not just from his or her own supervisor but also from other researchers in the environment and wants to get an overview of the research intensity of the institution, rather than just the immediate research group he or she will probably already be informed about. Again, the range across Europe will be considerable: the test sample suggests that 30% of institutions have very low research intensity, with hardly any peer-reviewed publications and less than 5% of their income for research. Only 40% of higher education institutions have over one peer-reviewed publication per academic staff member per year and over 15% research income. If doctoral students seeks a wider environment of research stimulus, the smaller group of institutions with more than two publications per academic staff per year may appear more lively in this respect. The overall percentage of the institution's income which is dedicated to research (Fig. 7.3) may serve as another

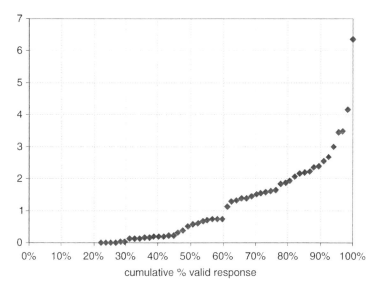

Fig. 7.2 Higher education institutions by the number of peer-reviewed publications per academic staff member

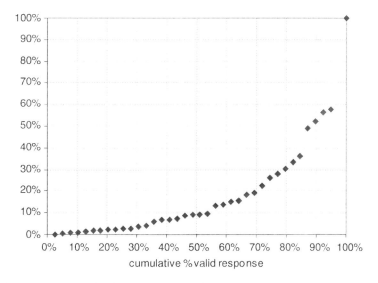

Fig. 7.3 Higher education institutions by research income as a percentage of total income

indicator of relative research intensity to corroborate the picture of the institutional profile in this dimension.

Finally, prospective doctoral students may be innovation disposed and may want to know how vibrant the research environment is from the point of view of

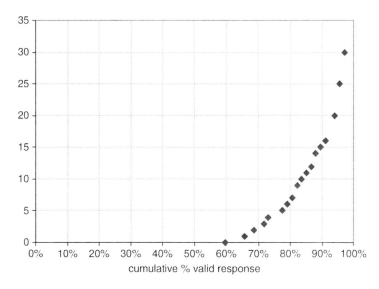

Fig. 7.4 Higher education institutions by number of start-up firms (annual average over last 3 years)

commercialisation and business opportunities, such as start-ups. A high intensity of start-ups would be likely to imply corresponding support services and resources which may be relevant for a student's potential initiatives. Here, European institutions show an even wider range of activity levels, as the test results of the classification suggest (Fig. 7.4). While 60% of sample institutions had no such activities at all, a small number was highly active, reflecting very different environments in this respect.

Researchers may be equally interested in the above-mentioned data comparisons of institutional activity. In addition, when being asked to join a particular institution, for example, they may also be interested in comparing their research resource and support environment with other institutions in Europe. To know, for example that, while over 50% of the higher education institutions receive less than 10% of their research revenues from EU research contracts, you are being invited to join one of the few where more than 50% of the turnover comes from EU research contracts, is important since it may imply certain expectations of your own time investment into EU applications (Fig. 7.5). Such data may also raise questions regarding the research resources available from the institution for infrastructure, maintenance, or as seed money. Similarly, a high degree of research resources from private sector contracts (Fig. 7.6) reflects particular institutional responsiveness toward business concerns. When seen in comparison to the overall institutional range in Europe, such data may become particularly telling. If the prospective institution obtains around 70% of its research revenues from private sources, for example, as is the case for one institution in the test sample, this reflects an institutional profile which is strongly business-facing. A researcher interested in optimal support for applied research and innovation will find a particularly responsive institution here, with a whole range of research support services adapted to IP and contractual questions, whereas one that is most interested in blue-sky basic research would be part of a minority here, which may raise questions as to the relevant support conditions available, e.g. for help in submitting research council and EU research applications. Coupled with the peer-reviewed publication record, such data sets will provide a first sense of the overall mix of research and innovation functions of the institution in comparison to the European spectrum.

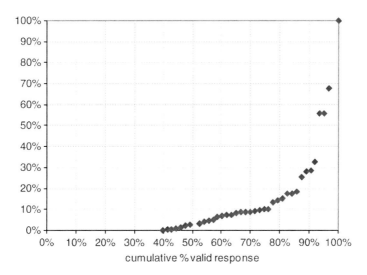

Fig. 7.5 Higher education institutions by revenues from EU research programmes as percentage of total research revenues

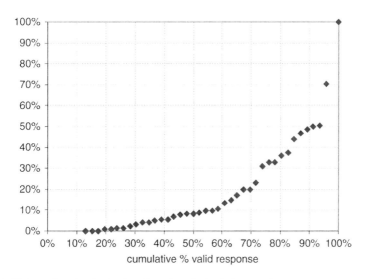

Fig. 7.6 Higher education institutions by privately funded research contracts as percentage of total research revenues

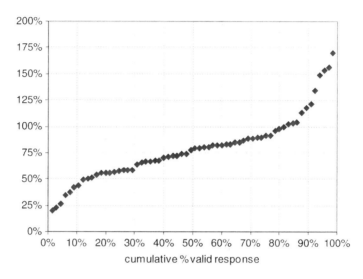

Fig. 7.7 Higher education institutions by ratio non-academic/academic staff

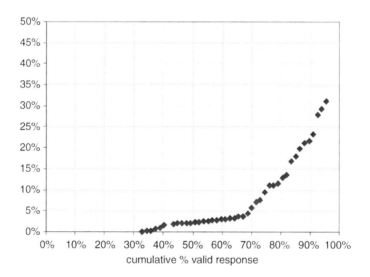

Fig. 7.8 Higher education institutions by percentage of international academic staff

A prospective researcher may also be interested to find out about the ratio between academic staff and non-academic support staff (Fig. 7.7). If comparatively low, it may be worth asking about the support available for research functions. If the researcher is interested in working in a relatively international environment, he or she may want to compare the institutional ratio of international academic staff with those of other European institutions (Fig. 7.8). While the vast majority of European higher education institutions have less than 10% international academic staff, it

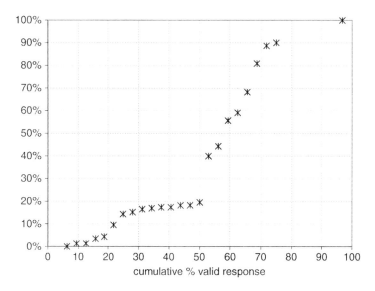

Fig. 7.9 Higher education institutions by percentage of programmes offered as part-time programmes

would be interesting to learn if the prospective institution belongs to that majority or to the small group of institutions where more than 50% of their academic staff come from abroad.

For a company interested in a closer partnership with a given higher education institution for the purpose of continuing professional development of their staff, it may be interesting to find objective data which makes transparent how actively the targeted institution is engaged in delivery of distance learning or part-time programmes (Figs. 7.9 and 7.10) and how many part-time and distance learning students it actually caters for. Here again we find only a small group of institutions that stands out as being highly engaged in this respect, as the test sample suggests. Most institutions have only a small percentage of their provision catering for part-time or distance learners. Some of these may even be regarded as specialised in the sector, offering more than 60% of such programmes. Also the percentage of programmes the institution offers abroad, may be a relevant indicator of its international market success. Companies interested in research cooperation with an institution would rather look at the previously mentioned indicators to obtain an overall sense of comparative institutional activity levels in research and innovation. Additional indicators, such as licensing income and patents filed would add to the overall comparative profile of the institution which can be drawn.

Of course, such insights may also help institutions, or rather their leaders and managers, to obtain a comparative sense of their own position in the European higher education landscape. Institutional leaders and managers may become more aware, for example, of what it takes to compete with the most actively engaged institutions in a particular dimension of activity. They may become more realistic with

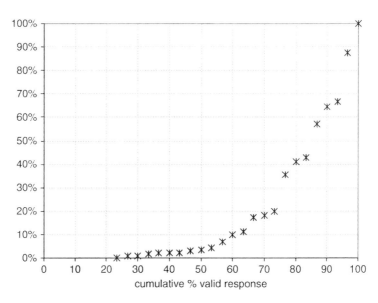

Fig. 7.10 Higher education institutions by percentage of programmes offered as distance programmes

respect to their own strengths and weaknesses through easier volume comparison with other institutions in Europe. Hitherto, international comparisons were only limited to some types of research output and to rather basic data on size of student enrolment and staff. Now, there will be not only be a wider angle onto such research output, but even more importantly, institutions may gain a more complete sense of their own position with respect to a whole range of activities, including innovation activity, programme range and international orientation. They may see more clearly the actual or desirable difference between the weights they place on particular parts of their mission from those chosen by other institutions. Higher education institutions can thus work on their institutional profiles, as the strategic orientations relate to their specific strengths and weaknesses.

To illustrate this point, let us take an institution whose leadership has believed it would be best to concentrate more resources on enhancing its international research profile. Such an institution may find out through the classification that its record with respect to peer-reviewed publications and research contracts is rather low. At the same time, however, it may see that it is very competitively positioned with respect to other aspects of international orientation, e.g. being one of the few institutions to offer 30% of its programmes abroad, having an above-average percentage of international staff compared to its peers (who may be more oriented toward teaching future high-profiles or business innovation activities than toward basic research), and as part of the upper 10th percentile of the most active institutions with respect to business research contracts, number of start-ups, etc. Such an institution could thus present a very convincing case to its key stakeholders and funding agencies of the competitive virtues of its own profile, arguing that it deserves financial support as a competitive institution facing an international market, even though it does not fit into the mould of the traditional basic research university.

From a systemic point of view, such readjustments of institutional priorities in light of comparative profile would be highly desirable since they would help to develop sufficient institutional diversity. Institutional diversity, which is necessary to sustain the diverse societal needs which have to be met by our higher education systems, is easily undermined in national and international contexts that are dominated by values relating to only one aspect of institutional functioning. That this is currently the case, with internationally published academic research being most highly valued in many higher education systems, has been widely commented on (see the previous Chapters 1–5). The European classification of higher education institutions offers a welcome new instrument that would allow international comparability and thus visibility of other aspects of higher education which have hitherto not been available. Since international visibility is becoming increasingly decisive for institutional profiling even in national contexts, the availability of instruments which would enable such visibility of other higher education functions is becoming an urgent issue. The mainstreaming of mission priorities is disconcerting for those who find that, beyond international basic research, other functions may be equally important. Indeed, the test survey confirmed that the spread of institutional identities may be unnecessarily narrow, with a vast majority of institutions, regardless of their institutional profile in different dimensions of higher education activities, finding research intensity the most decisive of the dimensions offered in the classification (Fig. 7.11). In contrast, regional engagement, professional

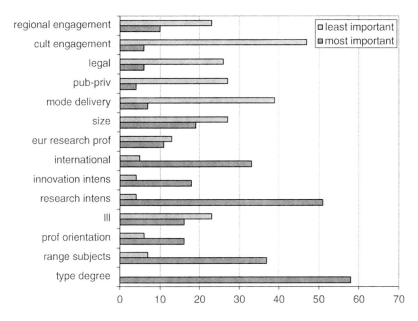

Fig. 7.11 Most and least important dimensions

orientation and innovation intensity were regarded as most important by very few institutions. Unfortunately the classification so far does not offer a dimension which would describe teaching activity in a manner that would allow it to act as a functional equivalent for research intensity. Thus, the respective priorities of the sample institutions cannot be easily derived from this first survey. But a forthcoming comparative study of five European countries on institutional diversity confirms an unnecessary concentration on research in institutional marketing behaviour and reward structures. The study shows that, even for those institutions which define themselves as primarily teaching-driven and show a remarkable volume and range of activities to cater for diverse teaching and learning needs, research is still the most highly placed criteria for hiring and promotion (Reichert 2009). Hence, international visibility of other functions is urgently needed to help broaden the focus and prevent a concentration solely on the research dimension of higher education.

The classification would also help higher education representatives, managers and observers, to distinguish institutional rhetoric from reality. For instance, if one is to take the rhetoric of international orientation seriously – which more than 90% of higher education institutions in Europe seem to espouse if one extrapolates from the test sample – this may require more efforts and investment than hitherto assumed. An institution that has disseminated an image of its international orientation among its members and stakeholders may find that it has to look for a more credible self-description and sense of identity if it finds itself on the lower end of the spectrum of European institutions in this respect, with less than 5% of its staff and less than 10% of degree-seeking students from abroad, less than 3% outgoing or incoming exchange students and hardly any programmes offered abroad, i.e. below average on all essential indicators of international orientation. Both for consumers as for institutional agents, rhetoric can be checked much more easily against reality if there is data that allows easy quantitative comparison across Europe.

For national policy-makers, these comparative pictures of institutional profiles may raise a whole new set of questions. Up to now, few policy-makers have been aware of the full extent to which institutions differ not only across national boundaries, but also within the same national context with respect to volume of activity. In particular, the more "marginal" but increasingly important functions of innovation, continuing education and regional engagement have not been made transparent in transnational and transinstitutional comparisons. Hence, national policy-makers will become more aware of the fact that competitiveness in and attractiveness of higher education do not have to be exclusively determined by research output. Such comparative transparency is likely to result in increased attention to other dimensions of higher education activity in which competitive positions may not have been as clearly known before, and in which progress and success may be more easily achievable.

Moreover, national policy-makers may become more aware of what it takes to compete with others internationally in a particular sphere of activity, including which targets can realistically be achieved, with what resources and in what time span. Indeed, up to now, there is little reliable data to show, for instance, the distribution of institutions with respect to the number of peer-reviewed publications,

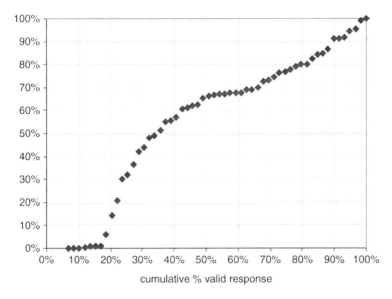

Fig. 7.12 Higher education institutions by percentage of government funding

number of start-up firms, average income for research or average income from tuition as a percentage of total income, nor even the range of institutional profiles with a breakdown of students at different degree levels. Without volume comparison, targets, and the estimates of resources required to achieve them, are often little more than mobilising fictions.

To illustrate the state of relative ignorance to which we are accustomed regarding basic facts of higher education, one may take the test sample data on the public or private character of higher education institutions. While it may be unsurprising that 70% of the institutions receive less than 20% of their research income from privately funded sources, we may be more surprised to learn that 30% of higher education institutions in Europe receive less than 50% of their income from government sources and that 40% receive more than 10% of their income from tuition income (see Figs. 7.12 and 7.13). In a Europe dominated by political rhetoric celebrating the public function of higher education, some discrepancies may be identified between these stated beliefs and the realities of institutional funding. Of course, the current data is derived from a relatively small test sample and should not be regarded as representative yet, but once the classification data schemes become established, such revelations will become possible.

Furthermore, once relative positions of institutions and systems on different dimensions are known, and targets have been set more realistically than was previously possible, reliable monitoring will also become possible. One will be able to trace over time how the efforts of one institution or system to increase volume of activity in a given respect compares with those of others. In an age where regions and nations seek to attract knowledge workers and knowledge-based companies

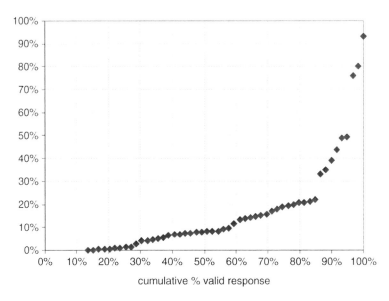

Fig. 7.13 Higher education institutions by tuition fee income as percentage of total income

as well as foreign direct investment in regional or national developments, the comparative volume increases of a national system may be welcome indicators of increased capacity or success.

For observers of the European Higher Education Area, the most exciting per-spective offered by the classification relates to the possibilities it offers to elucidate correlations between different types of higher education activities. One may see, to give just one example, whether and to what extent the volume of innovation acti-vity relates to volume of research activity, or whether high levels of innovation activities necessarily go hand in hand with more regional engagement or continuing education activities, as is often assumed. On the basis of such patterns, new ques-tions regarding the determinants of such interrelations may arise. For individual studies, such volume data may also be used to underpin more far-reaching data and inquiries into higher education activities and institutional behaviour. Increasing or decreasing levels of activity may be traced over time and may pose questions regarding the resources and choices that have shaped such developments.

7.5   Conclusion

Assessing the potential use of the European higher education classification by vari-ous categories of actors, the conclusion must be that the classification can be a major instrument for the further development of the European Higher Education Area. The classification makes the European higher education scene more transparent and allows its institutional diversity to become visible. In addition, it provides all kinds of strategically relevant information for many stakeholders: students, academics, business and industry, policymakers and certainly also the higher education institutions themselves. It helps these various stakeholders to make realistic and well-informed choices.

However, given the range of opportunities offered by the classification, one should also be aware of its limits and possible misuses. As an indicator-based scheme, the classification can naturally only achieve limited transparency: it seeks to reflect the measurable volume of activity in as many dimensions of institutional activities as possible, which in itself is a highly ambitious goal, given the complexity of the European Higher Education Area. However, as ambitious as this project is, it cannot achieve more than to provide a quantitative picture of institutional provision. It can reflect volume in diverse respects, but it cannot pretend to reflect quality. While volume may be related to quality, the two are not necessarily related. Hence, users of the classification would be reductive in their argumentation, even irresponsible, if they pretended to be able to use the classification to access the *quality* of higher education in a given system or institution.

This does not mean, of course, that measuring volume of activity or output is not already a highly helpful source of information, as pointed out above. But it cannot and should not replace the deeper qualitative judgements that are necessary to guide institutional and individual behaviour. Additional information on programmes, research content and quality, teachers and researcher profiles will be needed to inform the choices and judgements of individuals. Institutions and policy-makers need to see the value of the output as well its relation to resources, constraints, and regional and disciplinary contexts to understand the full quality of an institution. The European higher education classification does not want to replace these qualitative judgements. Instead it helps prepare these judgements by providing a wider quantitative insight into institutional profiles, which facilitates the formulation of helpful questions.

Some deeper questions remain and will remain unanswered for a number of years after the establishment of the European higher education classification. Most importantly, one may ask how such increased transparency with respect to institutional diversity will affect the latter. Will increased transparency on diversity of higher education activities and institutional profiles contribute or even increase diversity of provision by allowing monitoring and by designing targeted policy instruments to set sufficient incentives for the whole range of higher education activities? Or will some functions of higher education, such as internationally oriented research, remain so much more highly valued that the classification will mainly be used to add to the existing data on this dimension (presumably research) and be otherwise ignored? Will institutional leaders and higher education systems compare themselves with the already established prestigious institutions in the European landscape and strive to imitate them or will multiple markets and multiple frameworks of inter-institutional reference emerge, as is the intention of the classification?

As argued in the first chapters of this book, the existing literature seems to suggest that some government regulation or at least strong incentives are needed to counteract value-based mainstreaming and the resulting process of increasing homogeneity. At the same time, the dominance of traditional academic values is not cast in stone and may be mitigated by the confluence of alternative academic values which would allow for multiple orientations of higher education institutions, even emerging from within if sufficient support is also offered from above or from external sources. However, for such diversity of values to emerge, strong signals have to be set, ranging from financial incentives to symbolic recognition. The European higher education classification can provide the first step of making the whole range of higher education activities visible across borders. A decisive role will be played by those who use such information, institutional leaders and policy-makers who are ready to build on more transparent information in order to design differentiated incentives, so as to enhance the European Higher Education Area across all its dimensions.

References

CHEPS. (2008). *Mapping Diversity. Developing a European Classification of Higher Education Institutions*. Enschede: CHEPS.
Department for Education and Skills (UK). (2003). *The Future of Higher Education*. Presented to Parliament by the Secretary of State for Education and Skills by Command of Her Majesty, January 2003. http://www.dfes.gov.uk/hegateway/uploads/White%20Pape.pdf
Douglas, J.A. (2004). The Dynamics of massification and differentiation: a comparative look at higher education systems in the United Kingdom and California. *Higher Education Management and Policy* 16(3), 9–35.
Guri-Rosenblit, S., Sebková, H. & Teichler, T. (2007). Massification and diversity of higher education systems: interplay of complex dimensions. *Higher Education Policy* 20, 373–389.
Huisman, J., Meek, L. &Wood, F. (2007). Institutional diversity in higher education: a cross-national and longitudinal analysis. *Higher Education Quarterly* 61(4), 563–577.
Reichert, S. (2009, forthcoming). *Multiple Approaches to Institutional Diversity in European Higher Education*. Brussels: Publications of the European University Association.
Stjernø Commission Report. (2008). *Sett under ett. Ny struktur i høyere utdanning*. Oslo, Norges: off in Hige utredninger.
Veltz, P. (2007). Faut-il sauver les grandes écoles? De la culture de la sélection à la culture de l'innovation. Paris: Presses de Science Po.

Chapter 8
Using the Classification in the European Research Area

Christiane Gaehtgens and Rolf Peter

8.1 Introduction

The development of the European Research Area (ERA) has, like the creation of the European Higher Education Area (EHEA), clearly contributed to the growing attention given to institutional diversity of higher education in Europe. At first glance, the integration of Europe's research capabilities and the ongoing diversification of the European higher education landscape seem to be two processes leading in opposite directions and therefore hardly compatible. However, both initiatives, ERA and EHEA, are a challenge to universities, encouraging them to develop individual profiles that respond to the strengths and ambitions of the individual institution.

The idea of implementing the ERA, mainly driven by the European Commission, and the endeavours of institutional profiling, mainly driven by higher education institution leaders, are therefore not contradictory to each other. Actually, both processes are rooted in and spurred on by the same developments at systemic level. Globalisation – understood in this context as accelerated technological progress, internationalisation of markets and innovation systems – creates the need for the European Union (EU) as well as every higher education institution in Europe to respond to challenges to their competitiveness.

Undoubtedly, one of the ERA's main objectives, namely to overcome fragmentation and lack of coordination in European research (European Commission 2000), is put to the test by increasing institutional diversity. In Europe, internationally competitive research activity takes place in large superstructures as well as in small, insufficiently-funded university departments; it can be publicly or privately funded; its purpose may be purely blue-sky or decidedly applied, often with a focus on the needs of regional industry. Research policy and funding schemes vary considerably in the member states, and even though peer review is widely accepted there is no agreed common standard for quality assurance. If this diversity is to be an asset, i.e. a strength of Europe corresponding to the different and complex needs of modern knowledge societies, it needs to become transparent in all the aspects that determine the future competitiveness of institutional research infrastructure (Bartelse & Van Vught 2007). ERA will only be able to tap the full potential of Europe's research and innovation capabilities if all stakeholders, i.e. the universities and research institutes as chief actors, the stakeholders in business, industry and society and in particular the political architects of European integration, understand the nature of institutional diversity.

In the following it will be argued that a European classification of higher education institutions may help ERA to become a reality. It can provide a tool to overcome the prevailing fragmentation of the European research landscape, because it enables a variety of stakeholders to make more efficient use of Europe's research and innovation potential by:

- Creating transparency, i.e. providing systematic information and knowledge about the research profiles of European higher education institutions
- Facilitating inter-institutional and inter-sectoral cooperation
- Fostering research excellence at higher education institutions
- Supporting effective policy-making and coordination

Discussing the opportunities offered by a European classification of higher education institutions inevitably includes depicting its limitations as well. Obviously, the impact of such a classification on ERA will depend on a number of different factors – intrinsic and extrinsic. These factors range from the methodological design of the classification to the ability of European higher education institutions to effectively voice their interests in the political process of shaping the ERA.

8.2   Institutional Diversity: Feature of the Integrating European Research Landscape

The final years of the twentieth century saw increasing global awareness of the fact that economic and social development will depend essentially on the production, acquisition and use of knowledge in its different forms. Universities are at the heart of the so-called "knowledge triangle" providing education, research and innovation. More and more, their activities are for the express purpose of meeting social demand and satisfying social needs.

Against this background, institutional diversity, referring to differences in types of institutions within a higher education system, is often seen as a crucial factor associated with the positive performance of higher education systems. Diversified higher education systems are believed to produce higher levels of client-orientation (regarding the needs of students, the labour market, other stakeholders and societal interest groups), social mobility, effectiveness, flexibility, stability and innovativeness (see Chapter 1). Many national governments have designed and implemented policies to increase the level of diversity of their higher education systems.

From a political standpoint, the European higher education system's assumedly wide diversity is argued to be a highly relevant condition for the system's future development. Demand on the higher education sector is growing and widening in scope, from training a proportion of up to 50% of each age-cohort, initial academisation and lifelong learning to large-scale, highly competitive fundamental and applied research, knowledge transfer and innovation for economic growth.

But it is also the higher education institutions themselves, led by their leaders and governing bodies, that have been developing strategies to refine their missions and profiles in order to position themselves promisingly in the national and international competition for "brains" and funds. In this sense, the growing institutional diversity is mainly a bottom-up process. This process is likely to gain even more momentum as higher education institutions are granted more autonomy and accountability by their governments.

However, empirical knowledge about and transparency of the institutional diversity of European higher education is still rather limited. From the outsider's perspective of another institution, a student, industrialist or policy-maker, it is often difficult to identify, let alone compare institutional missions and achievements. Defining categories in which institutions can be recognised and compared by their aims and ambitions is a prerequisite for fruitful inter-institutional and inter-sectoral cooperation, competition, mobility of students and staff and relevant policies.

While the concept of institutional diversity has been widely recognised as a fundamental characteristic of the European higher education landscape, Europe struggles to create integrated Higher Education and Research Areas in order to meet the challenge of transatlantic and Asian competitors. And it is probably in the process of creating the ERA where the need for transparency is most essential.

8.3 The European Research Area

In March 2000, the EU and its Member States formally recognised that knowledge is Europe's most valuable resource and that Europe's ability to sustain a competitive edge in knowledge and innovation is crucial to creating the conditions for socio-economic development and long-term prosperity. At that time, the Lisbon European Council, on the basis of a corresponding Communication of the European Commission, endorsed the objective of creating a European Research Area as a core element of the European knowledge society (European Commission 2000). Such a society is supposed to be one "where research, education, training and innovation are fully mobilised to fulfil the economic, social and environmental ambitions of the EU and the expectations of its citizens" (European Commission 2007).

The ERA mainly constitutes a policy-driven top-down approach, a regulatory framework conceived and elaborated by the European Commission as a major vehicle to implement the EU's declared ambition to achieve a genuine common research and innovation policy. The ERA concept encompasses three interrelated aspects:

- A European "internal market" for research, where researchers, technology and knowledge can freely circulate
- Effective European-level coordination of national and regional research activities, programmes and policies and
- Initiatives implemented and funded at European level

According to the main documents issued by the European Commission (European Commission 2000, 2002, 2007), the ERA aims to:

- Facilitate academic mobility and attract the best researchers to European institutions
- Improve access to and use of knowledge throughout Europe
- Enhance the performance of European research institutions
- Foster inter-institutional and inter-sectoral cooperation in research and development and
- Establish a strategic policy planning process at regional, national and supranational level and creating a joint European research agenda

Looking at the ERA today, one has to conclude that some progress has been made along all three action lines during the last 8 years. Notably, the funding of the EU Research Framework Programmes (FPs) has been substantially increased, from a budget of nearly €15 billion for FP5 to nearly €54 billion for FP7. While the former FPs appeared to be no more than an additional research policy, coming on top of national regulative frameworks, "but not dynamic enough to have a truly integrating effect" (European Commission 2002, 8), FP6 and FP7 have been targeted explicitly at integrating European research, structuring the ERA and strengthening its foundations.

The newly-created European Research Council and European Institute of Technology have the potential to make a visible impact on the European research landscape and to strengthen the overall European science base. Furthermore, initiatives such as the European Technology Platforms and the so-called Joint Technology Initiatives, which are eligible for funding under FP7, offer frameworks for particularly ambitious research agendas in key technology fields that require a critical mass of joint public and private investment at European level. The ERA-Net scheme has been launched to improve coordination and networking of national research activities and programmes. Policy coordination is also addressed through the "open method of coordination" and the use of voluntary guidelines and recommendations. Finally, the EU has undertaken several steps in order to improve the framework conditions for research and innovation: e.g. it adopted a modernised Community framework for state aid for research and innovation; and the Structural Funds of EU cohesion policy give priority to the development of research and innovation capacities, particularly in less developed regions (Van Vught 2009).

Taking into account the goals and measures of the ERA, three main groups of stakeholders can be identified: private enterprises and their research & development (R&D) departments or institutes, publicly financed non-university research institutes and universities. Interestingly enough, in the beginning of the ERA policies universities played a subordinate role in the planning of the Commission and the Member States compared to industrial and non-university research centres (Duda 2008). It is only gradually that the Commission's interest in European universities has been growing. In three subsequent communications (2003, 2005 and 2006) it acknowledged that the European universities, "situated at the crossroads of research, education and innovation, […] in many respect hold the key to the knowledge economy and society" (European Commission 2003, 4). This seemed a coherent conclusion given the fact that in 2003 universities not only trained the next generation of European academicians, but also employed 34% of the total researchers in Europe and provided for 80% of Europe's fundamental research (Van Vught 2009).

At the same time the Commission remained critical of the performance of European universities. In a Communication from 2006 it concluded:

> In short: European universities are not currently in a position to achieve their potential in a number of important ways. As a result, they are behind in the increased international competition for talented academics and students, and miss out on fast-changing research agendas and on generating the critical mass, excellence and flexibility necessary to succeed. These failures are compounded by a combination of excessive public control coupled with insufficient funding. (European Commission 2006, 4)

In its 2007 Green Paper, the Commission restated the pivotal role of universities as a central pillar building the ERA, but also renewed its earlier critique. In reaction to the Green Paper, the European University Association (EUA) took up the thread in order to establish the views of universities on the issue (EUA 2007). The EUA embraced the Commission's initiative to re-launch the debate on the future development of the ERA and underlined the commitment of European universities to assume responsibility for themselves to become key players in the ERA. Yet the EUA also pointed out that the Commission should develop a more coherent approach in policies that concern European universities. The link between the different European policy domains where universities are involved (R&D, enterprise, regional development, external relations and others) would need better coordination Furthermore, the EUA expected the Commission to adapt and develop instruments of the EU's research and innovation policies, which are often more consistent with the needs and interests of enterprises and non-university institutions than those of universities, in order to enable the latter to establish themselves as key players in the ERA.

It becomes clear that the developments of both European universities and the ERA with regard to successfully meeting the challenges of globalisation are interconnected processes. Flexible, internationally networking universities with an individually recognisable research profile are crucial for the implementation of a genuine and viable common research policy in Europe. At the same time, in their efforts to sharpen their institutional profile European universities rely on a functioning ERA that not only provides a variety of funding instruments, but also a regulatory framework that efficiently coordinates resources and diminishes legal as well as administrative barriers to academic mobility, cross-border cooperation and public–private financing.

As of today the results of the ERA are best described as a mixture of success and underachievement. All the initiatives since 2000, and especially the launch of FP7, are valuable steps towards a genuine EU research and innovation policy and the increasing alignment of European and national policies. Yet – as the European Commission itself stated in its 2007 Green Paper "The European Research Area: New Perspectives" – much remains to be done to build the ERA, particularly to overcome the fragmentation that is still a prevailing characteristic of the European research landscape. Fragmentation puts up barriers to researcher mobility, inhibiting a free circulation of knowledge. It leads to difficulties in establishing cross-border R&D partnerships as well as to dispersing resources, because funding mechanisms and policies at regional, national and European level remain largely uncoordinated.

Moreover, it results in insufficient transnational coherence of reforms undertaken at national level and a lack of European perspective in developing science and technology. In short, fragmentation prevents Europe from fulfilling its research and innovation potential, at high costs to Europeans as taxpayers, consumers and citizens (European Commission 2007).

Addressing the question of how to overcome fragmentation and remedy its negative consequences, the Commission's Green Paper identified six fundamental features of "the European Research area that the scientific community, business and citizens need" (European Commission 2007, 2): a single labour market for researchers, world-class research infrastructures, excellent research institutions, effective knowledge-sharing, well-coordinated research programmes and priorities and international cooperation in science and technology. Expert Groups were set up for each of these six ERA dimensions. Their overall objective was to define possible measures and actions concerning the relevant ERA dimension, taking into account existing expertise, available evidence and the major elements stemming from the debate launched by the Green Paper.[1]

All Expert Groups started their work from the assumption that the still prevailing fragmentation of the ERA constitutes a major obstacle to its functioning. Taking a look at the findings of the Expert Groups, they more or less explicitly came to the concordant conclusion that fragmentation results, not least, from a lack of information and transparency. This is where the European classification of higher education institutions comes in. As a descriptive tool using principles of measurement, ordering and comparing, the classification will create transparency and reveal the diversity of European higher education institutions, which are the backbone of ERA. It will contribute to the reduction of complexity, and it may be used to identify multidimensional institutional profiles as well as institutional similarities and differences. Thus, the classification can be assumed to mitigate the problem of fragmentation and to provide added value not only to higher education institutions, but also to other stakeholders in European research and innovation, notably business and industry and governments.

8.4   Potential Impact of the European Higher Education Classification

In the following, we are going to further explore and test our main argument that the European higher education classification may help to make the ERA become a reality. It can provide a tool to overcome the prevailing fragmentation of the

---

[1] The list of Expert Groups (EGs) are as follows: EG 1: Realising a single labour market for researchers; EG 2: Developing world-class research infrastructures; EG 3: Strengthening research institutions; EG 4: Sharing knowledge; EG 5: Optimising research programmes and priorities; EG 6: Opening to the world: international cooperation in S&T. Additionally, a seventh Expert Group was tasked with developing and expanding "Rationales for ERA".

European research landscape, because it enables a variety of stakeholders to make more efficient use of Europe's research and innovation potential.

In order to test this argument, we need to come to valid statements about if/how the classification can possibly affect the main constituents of the ERA as defined by the European Commission (European Commission 2007, 2–3) and the responsible ERA Expert Groups:

1. An *adequate flow of researchers* with high levels of mobility between institutions, disciplines, sectors and countries
2. *World-class research infrastructures*, integrated, networked and accessible to research teams from across Europe and the world
3. *Excellent research institutions* engaged in effective public–private cooperation and partnerships, forming the core of research and innovation clusters and attracting a critical mass of human and financial resources
4. *Effective knowledge-sharing* notably between public research and industry, as well as with the public at large
5. *Well-coordinated research programmes and priorities*, including a significant volume of jointly-programmed public research investment at European level
6. A *wide opening of ERA to the world* with special emphasis on neighbouring countries and a strong commitment to addressing global challenges with Europe's partners

We are well aware of the prospective nature of our analysis. The European higher education classification is not established yet. Thus, our analysis will inevitably be future-oriented and, therefore, cannot result in "hard" proof based on existing empirical evidence. Nevertheless, the results of the case studies, pilot surveys and the survey described in Chapter 6 of this book, as well as the feedback from stakeholders, provide a basis for well-founded assumptions.

8.4.1 Realising a Single Labour Market for Researchers

The report presented by the responsible ERA Expert Group clearly shows that to develop a strategy that addresses the human resources needs of ERA, ensures more attractive careers for researchers and eliminates the obstacles hampering their mobility, is a complex, multidimensional endeavour (European Commission 2008a). The barriers to mobility are multiple, including lack of attraction, ethical recruitment and retention of researchers, lack of an equitable and cohesive social security system for researchers within the EU and lack of resources to cover the direct and indirect costs of mobility. Obviously, the European classification of higher education institutions is not the right tool to remedy all these deficiencies.

At a more general level, however, one could argue that lack of information is also a hindrance to mobility, since the ability of the individual researcher to make informed choices is a prerequisite for his/her mobility. The European higher education classification, presented in Chapter 4 of this book, provides information about an institution's research contents in terms of subject areas (indicator 2a), its research volume in terms of research income as a percentage of total income (5c) and its research productivity in terms of publications and number of citations (5a and 5b). Furthermore, researchers with a special interest in applied sciences and institutional links with industry can use the classification to compare the innovation intensiveness (number of start-up firms, number of patent applications filed, annual licensing income, and revenues from privately funded research contracts [6a–d]) of different institutions. Finally, the classification mirrors the international orientation of research at a given institution (international staff members as percentage of total number of staff [7c], income from European research programmes as percentage of total research income [8a]), which might be an incentive for a researcher looking for job opportunities abroad.

Taking a closer look at the dimensions and indicators, though, one has to admit that the classification is not primarily designed from the researchers' perspective or for their individual purposes. They would need, e.g. more detailed information from faculty and department level and will probably be interested in additional aspects such as living conditions or the general quality of life at a given destination. To this end, researchers have to use additional sources to satisfy their individual information demands.

Taking into account the complexity of the problem of academic mobility, the European classification of higher education institutions can only make a modest contribution to ensuring an adequate flow of researchers across Europe.

8.4.2   Developing World-class Research Infrastructures

According to the European Commission's Green Paper and the subsequent report of the responsible ERA Expert Group the "existence of and access to leading research infrastructures is and will remain a key determinant of Europe's competitiveness in both basic and applied research" (European Commission 2008b, 14).[2] As research and technologies advance, the demand for elaborate, increasingly complex and expensive research infrastructure is growing, thereby frequently overstraining the capacities of a single research group, institution, region or even nation. Against this background, a new strategic approach to the development of world-class research infrastructures across ERA is needed.

Given the need for state-of-the-art research facilities and critical mass on the one hand and financial constraints in the public and private sector on the other hand, networking and joint activities of research infrastructures in Europe has

---

[2] The ERA Expert Group defines "research infrastructures" as "facilities, resources and related services that are used by the scientific community to conduct top-level research in their respective fields. This definition covers: major scientific equipment or set of instruments; knowledge based-resources such as collections, archives or structured scientific information; enabling ICT-based infrastructures such as Grid, computing, software and communications; any other entity of a unique nature essential to achieve excellence in research. Such research infrastructures may be "single-sited" or "distributed" (a network of resources)."

already become a pressing issue. From the case studies and pilot survey discussed in Chapter 6 we received feedback from all participating institutions that identifying corresponding institutions in order to develop or expand partnerships is seen as a major benefit of the classification. By making their specific institutional profiles explicit and visible at a European level, higher education institutions make themselves and their research identifiable not only to other institutions, but also to non-university research institutes and R&D departments of private enterprises. This could facilitate networking, joint projects or even integration of existing research infrastructures across Europe, improve transnational access of researchers to these infrastructures and, thus, ensure their optimum utilisation.

However, it should be kept in mind that higher education institutions often play only a minor role in the current European strategies to set up research infrastructures of pan-continental relevance (see, e.g. ESFRI 2006). This is mainly due to the fact that higher education institutions lack the critical mass and the financial resources to substantially contribute to such voluminous projects. Although able to facilitate networking and cooperation between existing centres of research excellence in Europe, the European classification of higher education institutions will probably only have a limited impact in developing world-class European research infrastructures across the ERA.

8.4.3   Strengthening Research Institutions

As a result of its work, the responsible ERA Expert Group identified and defined possible measures and actions regarding the strengthening of research institutions with a focus on university-based research. This focus corresponded with earlier Commission findings that universities, although at the heart of the knowledge triangle, would not yet tap their full potential in the field of knowledge production and transfer for a number of different reasons (see above). From the Expert Group's point of view, strengthening research institutions basically means improving their research performance and is to be achieved by means of more institutional autonomy, better and more targeted funding and enhanced inter-institutional and inter-sectoral cooperation (European Commission 2008c).

By taking a closer look at the recommendations of the Expert Group it becomes clear that the classification can contribute to fostering the excellence of research institutions in the European Research Area. The Expert Group calls for more institutional autonomy that would allow European universities to specify their missions and sharpen their profiles: "They should be able to differentiate their activities based on their own strengths looking for excellence and relevance in strategically selected research areas or research domains at regional, national and/or international level" (European Commission 2008c, 6). Irrespective of the general need for more institutional autonomy, the feedback received from higher education institutions participating in the various research and discussion activities presented in Chapter 6 emphasises that a classification notably serves the need to sharpen institutional profiles. Institutions perceived the classification as a worthwhile exercise helping them to mirror and verify institutional ambitions and to design institutional development strategies. Similarly, many institutions participating in the survey (see Chapter 6) confirmed their interest in the classification, because it would enable them to identify relevant partners for benchmarking at a European level and thus help them to improve institutional performance.

Another recommendation of the Expert Group addresses cooperation and networking activities of European universities. More structured partnerships with other research institutions and the business community should be developed in order to create further opportunities for universities to participate in the joint production and application of knowledge. We have already referred to the way in which the classification is designed to make the research and innovation profiles of European higher education institutions more transparent and accessible. Stakeholders involved in the design process of the classification scheme so far have confirmed the scheme's potential contribution to the development of R&D partnerships between different institutions as well as between higher education and industry. Not only higher education institutions, but business and industry as well would profit from a tool facilitating the pooling of human and financial resources in inter-institutional and inter-sectoral R&D clusters.

The Expert Group identified serious under-funding as a core problem of European universities, with significant additional public investment required to ensure their global competitiveness. In this context, new competitive funding mechanisms at national and European levels which link research funding to performance are currently under discussion or already being implemented. Inevitably, the question of defining criteria for participation and evaluation of performance arises. Whereas existing international rankings usually appear to capture the prestige or reputation of higher education institutions, rather than their actual performance (see Chapter 5), the strictly descriptive dimensions and indicators of the classification capture the actual conditions and behaviour of higher education institutions. Thus, the classification may have an added value in formulating fair, effective research funding mechanisms for European universities and in the promotion of productive competition between them.

8.4.4 Sharing Knowledge

This ERA Expert Group on knowledge transfer addressed the access to knowledge generated by the public research base and its use by business and policy makers. In its report, the Expert Group formulated recommendations for improving knowledge-sharing in Europe in order to accelerate the utilisation of research and the development of new products and services. It thereby focussed on "the management and exploitation of intellectual property rights, primarily in the context of collaborative research, contract research and consultancy, company creation and growth, with a view to the increased use of knowledge maximising the benefits to the European economy" (European Commission 2008d).

In this sphere, the impact of a European higher education classification seems rather limited. Admittedly, by making research and innovation profiles of European higher education institutions more transparent and accessible, the classification would help make knowledge-sharing easier, quicker and more cost-effective to all stakeholders (business and industry, policy-makers, funding bodies, etc.). Yet effective knowledge-sharing in Europe involves more than finding suitable partners. The bigger part of the challenge lies in finding common ground between the partners. In order to ensure that all parties involved share realistic and reliable expectations about the fundamental terms on which publicly-funded knowledge is shared, common European standards and codes of practice must be developed and complied with.

8.4.5 Optimising Research Programmes and Priorities

Fragmentation in research efforts at regional, national and supranational levels prevents Europe from mobilising its full research capacities and capabilities. While science and industry are already far ahead not only in thinking, but in working across borders, European research policy has been slow to catch up. It is against this background that another ERA Expert Group focussed on how to ensure the coherence of European, national and regional research programmes and priorities as well as on improving coordination and cooperation between research and technology policies and programmes in Europe (European Commission 2008e).

As the Expert Group concluded in its final report, the limitations to effective transnational collaboration and Europe-wide policy coordination are rooted primarily in the strategic policy-making processes at regional, national and supranational levels, which are insufficiently interconnected. The Expert Group, therefore, calls for a strategic policy planning process at all levels that determines which instruments should be applied at which levels and which types and topics of research should be undertaken at supra-national level. The European higher education classification could provide detailed and systematic information to feed such a strategic policy planning process. It gives a substantial overview of what research is being carried out in Europe, in what subject areas and with what type of funding. This information is equally important to satisfy another need formulated by the Expert Group, that of identifying "joint visions, common goals and priorities on a European level that ask for a European approach" to research policy and programming. Common research agendas must be based on comprehensive knowledge of actual research performance in Europe.

The information provided by the classification can assist policy-makers in Europe to tailor policies and funding schemes aimed at helping different types of higher education institutions develop their specific research capacities and to promote a field and type (frontier, applied, etc.) of research. Such data would also support policy coordination at European level and help avoid dispersion of resources. This is one of the reasons why in 2008 the French presidency of the Council of the European Union, which had made better coordination of European research a priority on its policy agenda, showed particular interest in the classification project.

8.4.6 Opening to the World

The Commission's Green Paper explicitly related the ERA to the outside world by recognising that the EU cannot be a self-sufficient entity in the realm of science, technology and innovation. In order to progress, the ERA would have to meet two parallel challenges: deepening integration within the EU while also successfully interacting with other parts of the world. Knowledge generated in Europe is, in fact, utilised and disseminated worldwide and can benefit from developments occurring in North America, Asia and elsewhere. The challenge of interacting with the external environment was addressed by a separate ERA Expert Group (European Commission 2008f).

Aiming at coherent and effective cooperation with the outside world, the Experts Group's findings and recommendations to a large extent "externalise" those conditions and features which are also assumed to be vital for the successful integration of research activities within the EU: unhindered circulation of researchers, development and optimal utilisation of research infrastructure, enhanced knowledge-sharing, notably between public research and industry, and better policy coordination with regard to external research collaboration.

To this end, the classification can make the ERA's contribution to the generation and application of knowledge more visible beyond the borders of the EU. Additionally, the envisaged collaboration of a European higher education classification system with similar classifications in other countries or regions, such as the Carnegie classification in the USA, may serve the goal to establish "a more comprehensive information system on science and technology opportunities and perspectives" (European Commission 2008f, 92) at an international level.

8.5 Conclusion

Summing up the findings of our analysis, the European classification of higher education institutions may support the development of ERA in a number of ways. It could:

- Create transparency by providing systematic information and knowledge about the research profiles of European higher education institutions
- Facilitate inter-institutional and inter-sectoral cooperation by helping to make informed choices of appropriate R&D partners
- Foster research excellence at higher education institutions through encouraging productive competition by helping them to benchmark their own position in the European context, to define their goals in institutional development and to measure the progress they are making
- Support targeted policy-making and a better coordination of research policies and programmes at different levels in Europe

The classification can be used primarily by higher education institutions, but also by other stakeholders, notably business and politics, in order to derive higher benefit from Europe's diversity and make better use of Europe's research and innovation potential:

- Higher education institutions can draw on the classification to elaborate institutional research profiles and foster research specialisation. Against this backdrop, the classification can contribute to the process of internal quality development. Additionally, it can assist these institutions in forming cross-border R&D clusters which ensure high quality and critical mass, but at the same time allow for pooling human and financial resources.
- Business and industry can exploit the categorised information offered by the classification to identify the institutions they wish to relate to with respect to commissioning research and organising knowledge transfer across Europe.
- Policy-makers at national and European level can profit from the classification, because it may enable them to "tailor" policies targeted at different types of higher education institutions in order to develop their specific research and innovation capacities. Moreover, it can help them to establish a transnationally coherent system of (competitive) research funding that avoids dispersion of resources and excessive duplication of funding schemes.

The European higher education classification, thus, clearly responds to the strategic aims of the ERA, but it must not be overstretched if it is to meet appropriate expectations. The possible impact of the classification on the dynamics of ERA is limited by a number of factors, both intrinsic and extrinsic.

First of all, the descriptive approach of the classification rests on quantitative data and therefore does not fully address the quality of research at a given institution. It can only give "informed hints" as to where high-quality research is conducted. Qualitative dimensions can be covered only indirectly, although they play an important role in the development of the ERA. Quality of research is represented by indicators such as the number of reviewed publications and the scale of research funding from international sources. It is obvious that this gives a good indication of where a university's ambitions lie, yet this information will not be sufficient as a basis for strategic decision-taking.

The classification can only add to, and not replace, more qualitative analysis both at political and institutional levels. It must be complemented by evaluation procedures and other means of quality assurance for research by subject area, based on peer-review and geared to the decision-making of higher education institution leaders, funding institutions, companies and policy-makers.

Another limitation on the classification's potential impact not only on the ERA, but in general, arises from the fact that the interests of different stakeholders in using the classification tool may be contradictory and conflicting rather than in line with one another. This scenario is most likely to materialise with regard to the interests of higher education institution leaders and public authorities. Higher education institutions rightly perceive themselves as the most important stakeholders, not least because they provide the data. The prospect that the information provided by the classification might be used for political policy-making is a controversial topic among European higher education institutions, mainly because of their fear that institutional rankings, based on tailor-made subsets of institutions within the classification, might be "misused" as policy instruments. This is not the place to further elaborate on this issue, but it is clear that conflicts of interest may arise in the use of the classification, which in turn could negatively affect the development of the ERA.

Finally, it is not foreseeable, if or to what extent the classification will be able to influence organisational and individual behaviour in the ERA. Much will depend on the legitimacy of the classification, which, in turn, particularly depends on its acceptance by higher education institutions in Europe. Another related question is how the classification will be institutionalised and if its institutional implementation will exhibit a substantial level of inclusiveness, independence, professionalism, sustainability and, again, legitimacy (CHEPS 2008, 32).

Returning to our starting point, the interconnection between institutional diversity and the integration of the ERA, it might be worthwhile to underline once more that the classification does not take a position on what a "good" research institution looks like, but consciously restricts itself to providing a descriptive tool. By contrast, a number of experts and agencies at European and national level have recently expressed their opinions on the priority areas in institutional profiles that should be encouraged as they can be expected to compete successfully in the international race for excellence in research. Certainly, a driving force of the ERA is competition, both for input (eligibility, research funding) and for output (publications, patents, researchers attracted to the institution, etc.). Provided that the recommendations by ERA Expert Groups will be taken up by the European commission, the "rules of the game" and the standards for institutional profiles, which best fit these rules, have been set and will be communicated to the research community. It is to be expected that many major research institutions will strive to meet these standards in order to be successful in securing substantial amounts of European research funding and the increase the reputation that comes with it.

References

Bartelse, J. & Van Vught, F. (2007). Institutional profiles. Towards a typology of higher education institutions in Europe, *IAU Horizons* 13(2–3), 9–12.

CHEPS. (2008). *Mapping Diversity, Developing a European Classification of Higher Education Institutions*. Enschede: CHEPS.

Duda, G. (2008). The European Research Area and the European Higher Education Area: where do they meet and produce synergies? In: EUA Bologna Handbook.

European Commission. (2000). *Towards a European research area*. Communication from the Commission to the Council, the European Parliament, the Economic and Social Committee and the Committee of the Regions. 18.01.2000, COM (2000) 6.

European Commission. (2002). *The European Research Area. An internal knowledge market*. Luxembourg: Office for Official Publications of the European Communities.

European Commission. (2003). *The role of universities in the Europe of knowledge*. Communication from the Commission. Brussels, 05.02.2003. COM(2003) 58 final.

European Commission. (2006). *Delivering on the modernisation agenda for universities: education, research and innovation*. Communication from the Commission to the Council and the European Parliament. Brussels, 10.05.2006. COM(2006) 208 final.

European Commission. (2007). Green Paper. *The European Research Area: New Perspectives.* Brussels, 4.4.2007. COM(2007) 161 final.

European Commission. (2008a). *Realising a single labour market.* Report of the ERA Expert Group. Brussels.

European Commission. (2008b). *Developing world-class research infrastructures for the European Research Area (ERA).* Report of the ERA Expert Group. Brussels.

European Commission. (2008c). *Strengthening research institutions with a focus on university-based research.* Report of the ERA Expert Group. Brussels.

European Commission. (2008d). *Knowledge sharing in the European Research Area (ERA).* Report of the ERA Expert Group. Brussels.

European Commission. (2008e). *Optimising research programmes and priorities.* Report of the ERA Expert Group. Brussels.

European Commission. (2008f). *Opening to the world: international cooperation in science and technology.* Report of the ERA Expert Group. Brussels.

European Strategy Forum on Research Infrastructures (ESFRI). (2006). *European roadmap for research infrastructures.* Report 2006, Luxembourg.

European University Association (EUA). (2007). *European Commission's "Green Paper" on "The European Research Area: New Perspectives".* Viewpoint from the European University Association. Brussels.

Van Vught, F. (2009). The Europe of knowledge. In: D.D. Dill & F.A. van Vught (Eds.), *National Innovation and the Academic Research Enterprise: Public Policy in International Perspective.* Baltimore, MD: Johns Hopkins University Press.

Chapter 9
Using the Classification for Institutional Profiling: The Norwegian University of Science and Technology

Astrid Lægreid and Julie Feilberg

9.1 Introduction

Research and higher education are global activities that can be characterised by increased competition for human and material resources. The role of universities in the knowledge system has undergone important changes and universities are now and will become even more dependent upon their reputation, understood as perceived quality, influence and trustworthiness. In this context, it is necessary to rethink the way that we in universities evaluate our relevant activities and their quality.

This contribution first presents a brief description of the origins and profile of the Norwegian University of Science and Technology (NTNU) in Trondheim, and summarises our ambitions as formulated in our strategy. We then discuss the potential added value of the European higher education classification to our university's endeavour to achieve excellence and meet our strategic objectives.

9.2 NTNU: A Complex Institution

The roots of NTNU's history are grounded in Norway's first Academic Society, the Royal Norwegian Society of Sciences and Letters, which was founded in Trondheim in 1760, and which initiated the Museum of Natural History and Archaeology that much later became part of NTNU. Our recent history began taking shape with the establishment of the Norwegian Institute of Technology in 1910. In 1922 Trondheim was selected as the seat of the Norwegian Teacher Training College, which developed into the College of Arts and Science at the University of Trondheim in 1984. At this point, the broad academic base that would later characterise NTNU was mostly in place. In 1996, these institutions, together with the Faculty of Medicine, the Music Conservatory and Trondheim Academy of Fine Art, merged to become the present Norwegian University of Science and Technology.

A main driver for this merger was a strong political will in the Norwegian Parliament, which felt that NTNU should become a unique example of innovation

F. van Vught (ed.), *Mapping the Higher Education Landscape*, Higher Education Dynamics 28, 139
© Springer Science+Business Media B.V. 2009

among Norwegian universities. This was the first time that a main profile (Science and Technology) was integrated into the name of a Norwegian university. NTNU was thus given the responsibility for education and research in technology in Norway. The university was to provide full degrees and conduct fundamental research in its main profile areas, but at the same time, it was to remain a comprehensive university offering degrees and conducting research in medicine, the humanities, the fine arts and the social sciences. Another innovative feature assigned in the Parliamentary Charter was that interdisciplinary research should be carried out between the various disciplines and fields. These attributes of the university are reflected in NTNU's mission statement today which states that NTNU is to contribute to greater understanding of the interaction between culture, society, nature and technology, and to be an academic leader that safeguards and expands Norway's technological expertise.

Today NTNU is the second-largest university in Norway, with close to 20,000 registered students and 4,200 staff (full-time equivalents). Of these, 2,500 are academic staff and Ph.D. candidates. The university is organised in seven faculties with 53 departments and a Museum of Natural History and Archaeology. NTNU has an annual budget of €525 million of which approximately 75% is Norwegian state funding.

NTNU's main aims are to develop, maintain, create and disseminate knowledge in partnership with society, to develop expertise by providing students with a high-quality research-based education that has relevance for both the individuals and society. Furthermore, it is to renew society and contribute to wealth creation and better socioeconomic standards – regionally, nationally and globally.

NTNU offers programmes of study at all levels of higher education and has a broad academic scope with a primary focus on technology and the natural sciences. NTNU provides most of the graduate-level engineering education in Norway and offers an extensive range of subjects in the natural sciences, technology, architecture, the humanities, aesthetic studies, medicine, the social sciences, teacher training, and business disciplines. In addition to its focus on technology, NTNU has the broadest range of arts programmes offered at any Norwegian university. NTNU is also the leading Norwegian university in innovation and commercialisation of its R&D judging by the number of licenses and patents and the establishment of new companies.

NTNU's research has an international focus and can be characterised as being at the leading edge in specific areas of enquiry within all broad academic fields. Furthermore, NTNU has an extensive disciplinary scope combined with an emphasis on the interdisciplinary approach. NTNU has selected six thematic interdisciplinary strategic[1] areas that address key societal challenges where the institution is especially qualified to make a contribution:

- Energy and petroleum, resources and environment
- Globalisation

---

[1] http://www.ntnu.no/strategicareas

- Information and communication technology
- Marine and maritime research
- Materials technology
- Medical technology

NTNU is the host of three national Centres of Excellence[2]:

- Centre for Quantifiable Quality of Service in Communication Systems
- Centre for the Biology of Memory
- Centre for Ships and Ocean Structures.

NTNU also hosts three national Centres of Research-based Innovation[3]:

- Medical Imaging Laboratory for Innovative Future Healthcare (MI Lab)
- Structural Impact Laboratory (SIMLab)
- Centre for Integrated Operations in the Petroleum Industry (CIO)

To understand NTNU's activity and profile one must also understand the close partnership with the SINTEF Group based in Trondheim. SINTEF has a staff of 1,900 and is one of the largest independent contract research institutions in Europe. SINTEF performs contract research in technology, the natural sciences, medicine and the social sciences, and cooperates with NTNU in terms of staff, equipment, laboratories and scientific communication. Together, SINTEF and NTNU have established 21 Gemini centres for cooperation in selected fields of R&D. The partnership of SINTEF and NTNU has placed Trondheim on the map as one of the strongest technological research environments in Europe.

9.3 NTNU's Ambitions and Strategy

9.3.1 Why a New Strategy?

In the last few years NTNU has invested time and resources in a comprehensive process to define a more concrete, goal-oriented and ambitious strategy. The need for this has become increasingly clear among all constituent parts of the university, from students to academic and technical/administrative staff. Both external and internal factors have caused this awareness. However, external factors are generally seen to lend more urgency to the need for strategic goals and actions. NTNU emphasises its own impetus in providing a longer-term, pioneering vision of its future scientific potential, rather than merely responding to externally defined priorities.

NTNU needed to develop a more strategic approach in its dialogue with external collaborators in industry and the public sector, as well as in central and

---

[2] http://www.ntnu.no/excellence

[3] http://www.ntnu.no/researchbased_innovation

local government administrations and political bodies. Such strategic dialogue is a necessity because of the dual roles of our external partners – as employers of NTNU graduates and as potential sponsors of research projects and research in general. Also, strategic profiling in the national higher education landscape was increasingly necessary given recent trends towards institutional differentiation and the increased emphasis on achievement-based governmental funding. More focused strategic choices were necessary to compensate for possible reductions in government funding. Visualising a direct relationship between NTNU's institutional strategic priorities and those of the region and nation would contribute to securing goodwill and financial support.

Internally, our strategy development was influenced by the growing awareness that NTNU's activities must be characterised by excellence and that the achievement of excellence demands a carefully considered university strategy. Parallel to this, there was a growing consensus within NTNU that we had to prioritise our activities. Also we need to focus on internal initiatives and policies that will strengthen the quality of both research and education.

Where explicit regional or national priorities existed in terms of scientific or technologically focused areas, NTNU felt the need to define its position and not merely to respond to these priorities. More importantly, we needed to align these priorities with our institutional strengths and potential. In doing so we emphasised the need to foster synergy between different research fields, breaking down traditional borders between departments and disciplines. The NTNU strategy therefore contains a targeted approach to creating opportunities for cross-fertilisation among different disciplines in order to address urgent social problems such as globalisation or break new ground in medical technology.

9.3.2   NTNU's Strategy to 2020

NTNU's current strategy document was passed by its Board in December 2006.[4] Together with the 2001 strategy document entitled "Creative, constructive and critical" it forms our strategic basis.

Our vision is that by 2020 NTNU should be internationally recognised as an outstanding university. By means of generally accepted criteria and evaluation systems NTNU has set the following goals for 2020:

- To be among the international leaders in selected strong focus areas
- To be among the 10 leading technological and scientific universities in Europe
- To be among the top 1% of comprehensive universities in the world

It has been important in the new strategy document – "NTNU 2020, Internationally Outstanding" – to define concrete goals so that it becomes possible to operationalise them.

---

[4] "NTNU 2020 – Internationally Outstanding", http://www.ntnu.no/strategy

The strategy document describes NTNU, its role, values, vision and challenges. For each of the main areas: research, education, knowledge transfer, innovation and organisation and resources, the document formulates the university's overall goals and strategies as well as specific objectives for 2010 and 2020. Each objective is linked to key performance indicators. For the year 2020 the objectives are related to the European higher education and research areas, underlining NTNU's ambition to become internationally outstanding.

NTNU's key indicators include numbers of applicants compared to student places, mean grades for all admitted students, throughput of students at master's level and students' experience of the learning environment, number of Ph.Ds. awarded each year, scientific publications, external funding through contracts with user involvement and the number of companies being established as an outcome of the university's research.

The strategic objectives and indicators were chosen after a comprehensive and open internal process focused on how best to evaluate NTNU's development in the required strategic direction. Four or five key strategies were formulated for each of the main areas intended to give direction to the activities carried out in faculties and departments.

9.4 Profiling NTNU as a New Type of University

The initial merger creating NTNU resulted in an institution comprising different academic cultures with varying scope and approaches. While NTNU's profile in science and technology predominates, still the university cannot be classified wholly as a specialised technological university nor as a traditional, classical university, making comparisons with other institutions difficult. This contributes to a difficulty in clearly defining and communicating the NTNU identity both to internal audiences and to the wider community.

The emergence of NTNU represented a new entity on the university arena and a differentiation of the Norwegian system of higher education institutions. The new entity called for the development of a common identity and mission, which could exploit and build on the cultural and academic diversity of the institution and at the same time define and give the university a distinct profile externally. Striking a balance between competitive focus and sufficient breadth, comprehensiveness and diversity, is regarded as one of the most challenging issues being addressed and constantly reviewed in NTNU's strategy implementation process.

The significance of developing a distinct university profile should also be seen in relation to the characteristics of the Norwegian higher education system. In 2006, the Norwegian Government appointed what is known as the Stjernø Committee to assess the development of the higher education system in Norway. In their report, the Committee describes the increasing fragmentation in research and education across the higher education institutions, and a strong academic drive among the university colleges towards obtaining university status. The personal incentives of academic staff, furthermore, pull in the direction of traditional disciplinary research, which subsequently might be a detriment to professional studies. These developments combined may lead to a lower degree of diversification in the Norwegian higher education system than would be perceived as optimal for the society as a whole. The Stjernø Committee points to the fact that there is no national political strategy to counter developments towards fragmentation, low quality and productivity. This trend is also reinforced by the lack of interest in the national system by the individual higher education institutions.

Development of a high quality system of higher education and research, rather than hunting for a few world-class universities, calls for political and institutional strategies that create genuine diversity by counteracting fragmentation and by appreciating the different ways through which higher education and research institutions meet their societal responsibilities.

9.5   The Problem of Rankings

The process of developing NTNU's strategy has been important in order to define the distinct profile and identity of NTNU both internally and externally. But the process has also revealed certain weaknesses of operationalising societal responsibility and academic ambitions in terms of ranking.

Two facts are clear with regard to rankings. First, both the existing international rankings and the European higher education classification place NTNU within a global context. We are competing in the global arena for students, staff and money. Second, ranking systems are here to stay because there are strong public and commercial interests supporting their existence.

The most well-established rankings give surprisingly similar results, which increases their face value. In the most influential rankings, NTNU is ranked in the area between 200 and 300 in the world. While this is a result that would be considered satisfactory for many higher education institutions, our ambitions are far higher, as explicitly outlined in our strategy document.

Global university rankings have an increasingly strong impact on student and staff recruitment, on public opinion, and on important stakeholders. We therefore have to take them seriously into consideration. For this reason, NTNU has put a great deal of effort into a complementary approach, the European higher education classification, which, in our view, has the potential to enhance the value of rankings if employed before rankings are determined.

Despite the quality of the various ranking systems improving, few resources seem to be invested in the quality assurance of the data these rankings are based on. We have discovered inconsistencies and imprecise definitions in the various reports from rankings compilers, lessening the rankings' reliability. Some rankings change their indicators from year to year, making the ranking less suited for benchmarking a university's performance over a period of time. The leading league tables also seem to have a bias in favour of the natural sciences, technology and medicine and for publications in English. Furthermore, some give a lot of weight to an institution's reputation, while the same institution's contribution to society is given little or no weight at all (see also Chapter 5 of this volume).

The complexity of universities, their institutional organisation and their role, requires more sophisticated instruments of assessment than that currently provided by the existing university rankings. From the perspective of NTNU, there are numerous advantages in using the European higher education classification prior to ranking or other quality assessment.

9.6   The European Higher Education Classification and NTNU's Strategic Work

NTNU accepted the invitation to take part in the European classification project as a means of strengthening the strategic work that was already well in hand. NTNU was interested in assessment tools that place a greater emphasis on the relation between aims, strategies and achievements, particularly because of the use of performance management tools such as Balanced Scorecard in influencing government policies towards institutions of higher education and research.

In the following section, we discuss some important issues in working with a classification of higher education institutions, seen from our current perspective. Looking back on the experience gained by NTNU from working with the classification project, we will examine its contribution to NTNU's ability to work in a more strategic manner as an institution.

9.6.1   Strengthening Our Ability to Formulate Clear Aims and Strategies

In a competitive world, clear vision, aims and strategies are a prerequisite to the development and projection of a strong institutional identity and profile. This obviously cannot be done in isolation; comparison with others is a necessity. It is also vital to create a balance: we need to be seen as a university of high quality compared with similar institutions while also being seen as a unique university. It is therefore necessary to create a classification of higher education institutions that will enable us to compare with institutions of similar profile and aims. At the same time, the process of classification provides the opportunity to establish individual profiles by identifying features unique to some universities and not others. Existing international rankings do not provide the same opportunity. It could seem ridiculous for a mid-sized university on the outskirts of Europe to compare itself with the world's outstanding research universities. Such comparisons may even lead to possible 'fatigue', as it can be difficult to remain inspired by trying to compete in excellence with the very best. We can be inspired, however, by competing with peer universities, with similar profiles in research and education. By developing our strategic work, we will be able to identify a clearer profile, which in turn will enable us to compare ourselves with relevant universities throughout Europe.

9.6.2   Contributing to Our Discussions on Achievements

Clearly, good indicators are a necessity in measuring achievements and working with good indicators is crucial in all strategic work. For universities, with the acknowledged standards of academic work, this is hardly a new concept. The classification has obviously helped us in this regard. Not primarily by showing us new ways to assess and report results, but rather by boosting our confidence in what we have been doing. Furthermore, the classification can demonstrate that NTNU adheres to international standards for academic achievement.

9.6.3   Focusing on Our Priorities

As we stated previously, it is important to examine our results to measure the success of our strategies and gain new perspective on our aims and policies. A recurring and crucial question is whether we have given enough priority to NTNU's most important objectives. To look at it from a different perspective: should we prioritise aims that we can fairly easily achieve or should emphasis be placed on points where success is more difficult to achieve? Working with a classification process raises awareness of such questions.

9.6.4   Providing an Opportunity to Be Compared with Other Universities

There is an ongoing debate concerning whether competition between universities enhances academic quality or is instead a threat to academic endeavor, and to creativity and boldness in developing universities as institutions. We will not go into this debate here, because both views can be used as arguments for establishing means of comparing universities. The household word for this is benchmarking. There are plenty of benchmarking tools, but most are based on commercial thinking and are not best suited to universities. We want to measure quality because we want to improve our academic performance. For this we need relevant instruments. The European higher education classification is an attempt to establish standards that fit the need to classify institutions prior to any measurement of academic quality. We believe these standards are relevant to NTNU's strategic work, and will be acceptable to the academic community, an important consideration as acceptance from academic staff is vital to the success of the benchmarking.

9.6.5 Promoting Our Strategies and Achievements

Universities are operating in an environment where transparency is more important than ever before. It is not only funding bodies who want to know about our priorities and our achievements; the general public has an interest in and a legitimate need for this information, to be able to see how we stand compared to other institutions. Again, the relevant issue is benchmarking, the most effective and credible means of external audiences to assess university quality. In future, it will not be enough to rely on academic peer reviews to gain an insight into what defines quality in universities. The classification appears to offer a viable means to profile and highlight the multiple and complex dimensions that must be part of a quality assessment of today's universities.

A classification system should have the dimensions and indicators suited to differentiate between varying types of institutions, e.g., colleges and élite universities, and which may prepare for comparisons between institutions with similar profiles. Compared to current ranking systems, a classification system thus gives a better basis for developing a diversified higher education system and quality development and benchmarking.

There is a good match between the European higher education classification and the fields, objectives and categories that NTNU identified and prioritised in its strategic planning and implementation process. Thus, the classification captures NTNU's core activities and covers all important areas, with dimensions and indicators related to education, research and innovation and student, staff and institutional profiles. The classification will articulate NTNU's distinctive and institutional identity. The classification also reflects the societal function of a modern university like NTNU – the fact that universities' role as contributors to wealth creation in society has changed radically. The European higher education classification therefore contributes to NTNU's ongoing evolution and implementation of its strategic plan. We also appreciate the objectivity of the indicators used in the classification, which increases the reliability and value of the system.

9.7 NTNU's Engagement in the Classification Project

The classification project has been supported from the rectorate, which has represented NTNU at several meetings and conferences on the project. In addition, many senior staff with experience in the different aspects of the classification were involved in the site visit and provided feedback on the first drafts of the dimensions of the scheme and the classification tool itself. This broad involvement of senior NTNU staff members has had an intrinsic value, broadening our strategic competence and enhancing internal awareness of and enthusiasm for the coming system. Furthermore, the project management team was responsive to points we raised during the process.

In summary, NTNU has emphasised the following in its feedback to the project:

- The relationship between the classification and quality assessments should be clarified. The areas and indicators chosen in the classification are descriptive but may also imply quality judgments, i.e., the public may judge the quality and relevance of an institution using the classification, with thresholds per indicator interpreted as minimum quality levels.
- NTNU finds the areas selected – education, research, innovation, international outreach, regional and cultural engagement and institutional aspects – very relevant when considering its own profile. The success of the classification, however, will depend greatly on the robustness of the indicators. Clear definitions and a convincing standardisation are crucial. These can be obtained through in-depth definitions and a brief explanation of the intention behind each question.
- The data-gathering process should not overtax institutions' time and resources. Most of the data required by the classification corresponds to that required by the Norwegian government and already gathered in national registration systems, but some of the data required represents a challenge and will be time-consuming to assemble.
- Special attention should be given to the validity and reliability of the data via data audits (e.g., perhaps by national agencies such as existing accreditation agencies or statistics offices). Data should be available in public repositories.
- A crucial issue which needs further analysis is the way interdisciplinarity (both in education and in research) is addressed in the classification. In education, the "range of subjects" may imply a disciplinary bias. In research, a citation analysis approach may show a similar bias. It is important to find indicators that capture interdisciplinarity.
- As it may be senior staff members who fill in the data when the instrument is formally launched, it is important that the web version of the instrument should be user-friendly so as to facilitate data input as much as possible. It should be possible to store in draft format, so that the user can return to make corrections or complete data input without having to start again from the beginning.

9.8   Conclusion

In our view, the European higher education classification will help describe the diversified roles that Europe demands of its institutions of higher education and research. The European higher education classification is broader and more multidimensional than traditional ranking systems, making it more suitable to define an institutional profile. A classification system has the dimensions and indicators suited to differentiate between different types of institutions, e.g., colleges and élite universities, and which may prepare for comparisons between institutions with similar profiles. Compared to ranking systems, a classification system thus gives a better basis for developing a diversified higher education system and quality development and benchmarking.

There is a good match between the European higher education classification and the fields, objectives and categories that NTNU identified and prioritised in its strategic planning and implementation process. Thus, the classification captures NTNU's core activities and covers all important areas with dimensions and indicators related to education, research and innovation and student, staff, regional and cultural engagement and institutional profiles. The classification will articulate NTNU's distinctive and institutional identity. The classification also reflects the societal function of a modern university like NTNU – the fact that universities' role in contributing to wealth creation in society has changed radically. The European higher education classification, therefore, contributes to NTNU's ongoing evolution and implementation of its strategic plan. We also appreciate the objectivity of the indicators used in the classification, which increases the reliability and value of this new and promising instrument.

Chapter 10
Using the Classification for Institutional Profiling: The University of Strathclyde

Peter West and Saskia Hansen

10.1 Introduction

In this chapter, the experiences and aspirations of one European university, Strathclyde in Glasgow, are examined to see what practical value a European classification of higher education institutions would provide. Institutional rankings have developed more rapidly in the United Kingdom than elsewhere in the European Union and British universities such as Strathclyde have amassed many years of experience in dealing with the managerial consequences of league tables. For them, classification holds out the alluring prospect of being compared with like institutions within the rich diversity of European higher education.

The pressure to perform well in the institutional rankings is rising inexorably. Rankings have become so closely linked with both external reputation and institutional self-image that they can no longer be ignored. Yet they can easily pull an institution away from its unique mission, often aligned with the particular needs of the local community, towards the orthodoxy that secures league table success. Thus league tables are the enemy of diversity.

In 1993, Clark Kerr, President of the University of California and godfather of the American Carnegie Classification wrote this:

> For the first time, a really international world of learning, highly competitive, is emerging.... If you want to get onto that orbit, you have to do so on merit.... You cannot rely on politics or anything else. (Clark 1998, p. 136)

Sadly, league tables do not support this meritocratic vision. As has been argued in Chapter 5 of this volume, there is an in-built bias in the Shanghai Jiao Tong table in favour of large, English-speaking universities with strength in Science – in other words, those with an established reputation. In the United Kingdom, there are three sets of league tables based on entirely different data sets and weighting and designed for different audiences by three of the most respected newspapers in the UK – *The Times*, *Sunday Times* and *The Guardian*. Yet over many years, six universities have always appeared in the top 10 of every table published (HEFCE 2008). In 2008, the latest data showed that Strathclyde's entry standard, in terms of the qualification of new entrants, was the third highest in the United Kingdom. The league table compiler challenged this on the grounds that it was counter-intuitive.

F. van Vught (ed.), *Mapping the Higher Education Landscape*, Higher Education Dynamics 28, 151
© Springer Science+Business Media B.V. 2009

The figures were checked and validated, but the compiler simply decided not to use that measure. There is, without doubt, a significant measure of intuition, driven by established reputation, behind some of these tables. Indeed *The Times* and *The Guardian* explicitly say that final league table positions cannot be derived from the supporting data published.

The data underlying the two international league tables, *THE* and Shanghai Jiao Tong, is more robust, though even the latter has been challenged on the grounds that it is irreproducible (Florian 2007). A recent analysis carried out for the Higher Education Funding Council for England has demonstrated that these two tables have only a single source of data, numbers of citations, in common (HEFCE 2008). Yet they come to a broadly similar conclusion. Even citations are open to challenge since, as has been argued in Chapter 5, they favour American institutions, which tend to cite others' work to the exclusion of research in other continents.

The impact on institutional morale for a university such as Strathclyde, which does not perform as well in the league tables as it believes it should, is considerable. The impact can and does extend to whole systems.

European Commissioner Ján Figel (2008) commented at a conference in Brussels in February 2008 that Europe was not achieving the same global dominance in higher education as it was in football. Other European Commission reports have pronounced that European higher education is not globally competitive, this conclusion being clearly based on the international league tables. Implicit in these comments is the assumption that if institutions conformed more closely to the norms of the compilers, they would be more successful.

In other parts of the European Commission, it is increasingly recognised that universities have a key role to play in regional economic development and addressing social problems such as low participation rates in higher education by disadvantaged citizens. Metrics of successful economic impact such as spin-out companies and patents gain no credit in league tables, however, and measures such as flexibility over entry standards to widen access has actually cost universities places in some rankings.

If it is accepted that there is only one definition of an "excellent" university, it follows that all should aspire to it. New universities assume that in due course, if they get their strategies right, their profiles will grow and their reputations evolve until they achieve parity with the most ancient institutions of higher education. There are, however, important distinctions between being research-based and teaching-based and between higher education and skills-based training. The differences should be safeguarded. As Lord Krebs, Master of Jesus College, Oxford, put it in a debate in the British House of Lords in June 2008.

If my daughters came home from school and told me they had been to sex education classes, I would be comfortable; if they said they had been to sex training and skills classes, I would not (THE 2008).

Diversity should be encouraged – for the strength of the sector overall and the institutions and for the benefit of their constituencies. As Professor John Hood (2006), Vice-Chancellor of the University of Oxford, stated in a conference speech in 2006: "Every University needs to identify its unique mission and then be the best in the world at that."

The challenge posed by Professor Hood creates its own issues for universities. Without a reliable system of classification to validate its pursuit of diversity, how does an institution:

- Identify and engage in its unique mission?
- Establish to the satisfaction of governments and the public that it has a distinct mission from others?
- Measure its progress against comparable institutions elsewhere?
- Decide what would indeed be a world-beating performance?

The University of Strathclyde in Glasgow is one of the five particularly innovative European Universities chosen as case studies by Professor R. Burton Clark for his influential book *Creating Entrepreneurial Universities* (1998). Strathclyde has particular strength in engineering, sciences and applied sciences. Since its formation in 1796, it has had the same mission, highly unorthodox in its day, to be "a place of useful learning".

In 1993, the University of Strathclyde merged with Scotland's largest teacher-training college, Jordanhill, believing that this was fully consistent with its traditional mission of adding value and serving society. Sadly, teacher training is one of those subjects which do not achieve high recognition in the league tables. The immediate impact of the merger was to reduce the University's position in British league tables by about 10 places. At the time, this seemed a price worth paying but in 2006, the growing influence of league tables meant this effect could no longer be ignored. The Faculty of Education is being transferred to a new building alongside the rest of the University, new leadership has been brought in and research is being strengthened.

That programme forms part of a wider "Agenda for Excellence", which aims to address areas of weakness and consolidate areas of strength so that Strathclyde will become a place where "only the best are good enough to work and study". A place in the league tables which reflects Strathclyde's own view of its relative strength is one of the key outcomes that is expected to follow, but it will not be allowed to interfere with the University's unorthodox, particular mission of "useful learning".

10.2   Why Classify?

For the reasons outlined above, i.e. the global reputation race and the increasing predominance of league tables favouring traditional research universities, it has been part of the regular environmental scanning work undertaken by the University's Planning Team to identify developments that could lead to new opportunities for meaningful benchmarking or more systematic comparisons with other universities both in the UK and in the larger European Higher Education Area. While the league tables provide some measures for benchmarking, the rankings themselves do not reveal much information about the underlying differences or similarities between the institutions included. The project to design a European higher education classification was consequently well-aligned with an institutional interest in exploring and supporting alternative approaches to structuring the diverse higher education landscape outwith the realm of traditional rankings. Therefore, the University of Strathclyde was happy to join the project.

While scepticism was expressed about the project from some stakeholders across Europe, the University of Strathclyde welcomed this opportunity to engage in the project and to influence the development of the classification tool in a direction that was felt to be appropriate and suitable from a strategic institutional point of view. Similarly, through Strathclyde's membership of the European Consortium of Innovative Universities (ECIU), there was an opportunity to also feed back input from other ECIU institutions to the classification project team and to get a feel for how other countries in Europe perceived the usefulness of such an instrument.

10.3   Contributing to the Design of the European Higher Education Classification

As an outgrowth of its institutional interest in developing the European higher education classification, and following initial discussions about how best to gauge institutional needs, requirements and data availability, Strathclyde volunteered to become a case study institution. This involved organising a site visit that would give the project team insight into the University's potential use of the classification and would identify possible difficulties in producing the required data.

To give the project team a comprehensive understanding of the situation at Strathclyde and the external drivers with the greatest impact on the University's development, and in turn on its perception of the usefulness of the classification, meetings were organised with a broad spectrum of colleagues across the University, including the:

• Director of Marketing & Communications
• Research Assessment Exercise Project Manager
• International Office
• Communications Office
• Planning Team
• University Secretary
• Deputy Secretary

The initial discussions at these meetings, on the dimensions of and indicators used for the classification, provided a framework for comprehensive and in-depth reflection on what institutions that were to become active users of the classification might see as concerns in terms of data collection and analysis, and in terms of the indicators used to capture the diversity of higher education across Europe.

The main points captured in the case visit were:

- **Survey fatigue**

When the site visit took place, the University was in the final phase of preparing its submission to the government's Research Assessment Exercise 2008. This had involved substantial human resource across the University, and several members of staff working full-time on a database to prepare and organise the research data. As a result, there was comprehensive information on research income, publications and citations, indicators of external esteem and research student numbers – a wealth of research information that could be utilised for other purposes as well.

The University makes submissions to the UK Higher Education Statistics Agency (HESA) and the Scottish Funding Council on, for example, student numbers, student progression and student loads, graduate employability and staff numbers by category, and submits financial data on income streams and cost centres. Again, a substantial amount of work goes into data gathering and organising and filing these submissions. A strong recommendation, therefore, was that data used for the classification and data submitted to national agencies should be as closely aligned as possible. This would limit the burden on participating institutions and would significantly enhance the quality of the data used to populate the classification.

- **Reputation and competition**

The site visit included substantial discussion about the nature of UK league tables. Though the University remains sceptical about these league tables and the way they favour traditional, research-intensive universities, it has acknowledged that many students, particularly overseas students contemplating study in the UK, find them a valuable guide when deciding on the institution they believe will provide the best degree and student experience. League tables, whether the sector likes it or not, are consequently a force to be reckoned with and considerable time and effort is spent maximising every opportunity to improve a university's perceived performance. Ultimately, league table standings are linked with actual performance as measured through selected indicators such as retention and employability. Due to the weightings and indicators used in producing the UK league tables, however, an improvement in real-life performance might not always have a direct effect on league table performance, as Strathclyde has experienced over the years.

In 2008, the University of Strathclyde had the third highest Entry Standard in the UK, as HESA allowed the inclusion of additional qualifications in the submission, but *The Times* League Table would not accept this as a plausible outcome and therefore chose to not publish the data.

League table compilers are commercial providers and define the indicators and weightings used to rank educational institutions. While there may be an opportunity to influence the shape and form of the indicators through dialogue with league table editors, ultimately the higher education sector has no choice but to accept whatever the league table compilers come up with. To opt out of the league tables is simply not possible.

The University's International & Graduate Office and Alumni & Development Office are particularly aware of the knock-on effect of performance in league tables. Alumni in the Far East have at times questioned the University's strategic alliances with some partner institutions which do not show to advantage in the Shanghai Jiao Tong University China International League table. Strathclyde, however, had not chosen these collaborative partners on the basis of traditional research performance, but for their strengths in applied research, outreach and innovation; dimensions not captured in the typical league table. These alumni may not have picked up on the nuances and may have judged these institutions on the basis of league table performance only.

From this perspective, the European classification would be interesting as a more balanced measure that would better capture the diversity of higher education valued by the University of Strathclyde and others, while still providing a structure and a framework for comparing different universities that could be helpful to prospective students and alumni.

- **Strategic planning and horizon scanning**

The University had just approved its Strategic Plan 2007–2011 when the site visit took place, and discussions consequently touched on the crucial importance of environmental scanning, benchmarking and analysis of comparator institutions.

While Strathclyde had taken part in benchmarking and comparative analysis of technology transfer activity, entrepreneurship programmes, and administrative structures with other member institutions of ECIU, the Planning Team was aware of the lack of data in the broader European landscape that could be valuable in broader benchmarking exercises and for the identification of good practice.

A desired outcome of the classification therefore would be measures that could lead to cross-institutional European benchmarking.

- **Questionnaires**

As part of the early stage project work, Strathclyde had the opportunity to provide input to the pre-pilot questionnaires on dimensions and indicators (see Chapter 6).

As a recognised innovative institution branded "The Place of Useful Learning", Strathclyde appreciated the fact that the classification allowed for dimensions beyond the mere traditional, such as innovation intensiveness.

However, the Strathclyde Planning Team's involvement in responding to the pre-pilot questionnaires uncovered flaws in the questions:

- Two questions were at times combined in a single query (e.g. "percentage of programmes offered as distance learning or mixed learning"), with the response restricted to a single answer. This led to a lack of clarity in responses. Furthermore, it was not clear whether a 3-year degree programme with just one module offered via distance learning would qualify as mixed learning.
- Another question requesting "the number of extra-curricular courses offered for the regional labour market" did not define "extra-curricular", which could be

open to different interpretations in different institutions, and similarly did not specify what was indicated by "regional". The regional labour market for the University of Strathclyde could be Scotland in a broader European context, or the immediate West of Scotland area around Glasgow.

- The question "annual turnover in EU Structural Funds" is more relevant to certain institutions than to others. Eligibility for such funds is restricted to institutions in particular European regions only, which would lead to inaccurate capture of information, since it would not be clear whether an institution was, in fact, not based in a region eligible for funding or whether it was eligible but simply ineffective at making successful bids.

There were also some technical issues with the web-based user interface: a question and its response options could not be seen in its entirety on the screen, but required a respondent to scroll down; and there was no means of printing out responses, or indeed saving a response to return to it later.

These issues were duly addressed and the questionnaires circulated for the actual pilot test were substantially better than the pre-pilot questionnaires and web-based user interface.

- **Lessons learned**

From this early involvement in the project, Strathclyde formulated some key lessons learned and forwarded these to the project team.

10.3.1   Communications

Communication with key internal stakeholders at various stages is of critical importance. Because of the staff time involved in responding to the questionnaire, the Planning Team (or its equivalent) must fully understand the strategic importance of the task to their institution (assuming that participation is based on a senior management decision that the European higher education classification is relevant to their institutional objectives).

If the classification subsequently becomes a tool used by institutions and their stakeholders, promotion of the classification to staff and students at large should be clear and concise, explaining its purpose and how it differs from rankings.

10.3.2   Robust Questions and User-Friendly Interface

Again, as the credibility of the tool will depend on the integrity of the underlying data, the questions used should be straightforward, leaving no room for misinterpretation regarding the information being requested.

10.3.3   National Data Sources

Finally, the likelihood of institutions participating in the classification would increase substantially if the data requested were aligned with national data requirements. In the UK, this would mean that data submitted to HESA could be re-used for the classification tool.

The Higher Education Statistics Agency (HESA) provides a wealth of data about the UK Higher education sector. HESA is the official agency for collection, analysis and dissemination of quantitative information about UK higher education.

HESA was set up in 1993, following the White Paper "Higher Education: a new framework", which called for more coherence in HE statistics, and the 1992 Higher and Further Education Acts, which established an integrated higher education system throughout the United Kingdom.

A key recommendation arising from Strathclyde's experience in the European higher education classification would be to align data requirements and collection with data already collected and made available in national repositories such as the UK's HESA.

10.4   Moving Forward: Future Uses of the Classification

Within the context of Strathclyde's "Agenda for Excellence" and its aspirations for future development, the European higher education classification is seen as a tool that could underpin some of the strategies being deployed in pursuit of our objectives.

In particular, there are opportunities for use of the tool in the following four areas: analysis and horizon scanning; improving student mobility; matchmaking; and relations with employers.

- **Analysis and horizon scanning**
Awareness of the external environment is critical in terms of developing an institutional ability to anticipate and respond to developments. Strathclyde has regularly used systematic benchmarking to identify opportunities for performance improvement. Annual performance monitoring reports are produced and presented to the University's governing body, the University Court. However, these analyses have been restricted by the fact that data is only readily available for the UK sector, not for higher education institutions further afield. As competition for the best students and staff is global, it would be desirable to have better and more numerous sources of data on higher education in other parts of the world. The classification would allow for increased access to quality data and information about other institutions, which would further support Strathclyde's horizon scanning work.

If more institutions support this type of use of the classification, it would influence the way in which the tool is set up in terms of providing access to underlying data. Institutions providing data for the classification could be asked to share their data with other institutions. This would give added value to the classification for those institutions permitting access to their raw data and allowing them access to the data of other institutions.

Further consideration would have to be given to how this type of sharing of data could be encouraged and organised, but this potential use of the classification would be of particular strategic interest to Strathclyde.

- **Improving student mobility**

One of the key strategic objectives at Strathclyde is to increase the number of students incorporating study or internships abroad into their programme of study at Strathclyde. Higher education institutions across the UK struggle with the same challenge, as statistics reveal that proportionally fewer UK students study abroad than other continental European university students. If students do go abroad, there is a tendency to favour English-speaking countries such as Australia and the United States.

Strathclyde is aiming to increase the number of students taking a semester of their studies in Europe, and over the last couple of years the University has organised events and campaigns encouraging more students to considering studying abroad. However, surveys of our students, intended to identify the reasons behind low study abroad participation rates, consistently raise "lack of information about the opportunities" as a factor. Despite the range of information events, and materials in print and online about study abroad opportunities, it is clear that more or different information would be desirable from a student perspective.

Consequently, the University believes the classification may help in providing the type of additional information that students are seeking. It is clear that anything that can help boost student confidence in considering study at other European institutions and the prospect of encountering different languages and university cultures would be helpful.

The European higher education classification could be incorporated into the cycle of early-stage broad-brush information sought by students when screening Europe to see which universities might be of interest to them. The classification would not replace advice provided by academic supervisors, but could supply an interesting, complementary layer of information, allowing students greater insight into what characterises different institutions.

- **Matchmaking**

Strathclyde is well known in Scotland for its close links with business and industry as illustrated by a recent agreement with Rolls-Royce and other major industry players to establish an Advanced Forming Research Centre with significant industry investment. Strathclyde's Strategic Plan 2007–2011 outlines its aspiration to enter into two or more such strategic collaborations every year.

However, the University of Strathclyde also engages in various types of support to small- and medium-sized companies. Smaller-scale businesses often do not have the same R&D facilities as the major players and may at times approach the University for advice and input regarding potential European collaborators. With several European funding programmes requiring such collaboration with companies and higher education institutions elsewhere in Europe, any resource that can provide early-stage input to companies about possible collaborators could prove extremely useful.

Strathclyde has not tested in any systematic way the classification's potential direct use to smaller enterprises, but the tool could prove to be of practical value to the University's Research & Innovation Office as it supports the development of applied research projects between smaller industrial players and consortia of higher education institutions.

Clearly, more analytical work is required to identify the information requirements of this stakeholder group and their potential uses of the European higher education classification, but from a Strathclyde perspective it appears the classification could be relevant in these types of industrial matchmaking activities.

- **Employer relations**

Strathclyde's award-winning Careers Services and many of the academic departments have close links with the major employers in the West of Scotland. Some are represented on Advisory Boards and support curriculum development activities, and employers are considered important strategic stakeholders in that the University aims to produce high-quality, employable graduates.

However, in a global marketplace, more students may wish to go abroad for employment, or local employers may recruit graduates from other European countries. As with the industrial matchmaking idea, there are opportunities for employers to utilise the findings of the European higher education classification when considering job applicants from other countries. The Diploma Supplement (DS) has provided much-needed transparency and clarity on what different degrees mean in terms of abilities and skills, but does not provide much information on the institutions issuing the degrees. The classification may give a broader supplementary perspective to the DS by making available high-level institutional information.

Similarly, Strathclyde may be able to use the classification in its marketing materials. The University has a strategic interest in ensuring that its graduates find employment, and some of the material published about the University could utilise descriptors from the classification. Similarly, the statistical "spider webs" that can be developed on the basis of the information contained in the classification database (see Chapter 4) are useful visual illustrations of how the University scores on the different dimensions of the instrument (such as whether we are more or less innovative on average than other institutions included in the classification). Again, such illustrations could be used in the University's portfolio of marketing materials and may ultimately be helpful to prospective students when they consider whether or not to study at Strathclyde.

10.5   Conclusion

As the discussion surrounding league tables illustrates, these are challenging times for higher education institutions in Europe. The competition for students and staff is growing, and existing league tables and global rankings create an indirect push for uniformity: improvement in performance against a limited set of indicators is required in order to move up in the league tables. The values of diversity in institutional cultures and traditions are accordingly under threat.

A new European higher education classification would provide opportunities for better recognition of the diversity and differences in higher education institutions across Europe. It would permit universities such as Strathclyde to establish their position in the landscape of European higher education.

Action and reaction, we are taught in physics, are equal and opposite. Across Europe we see the pressure for financial and regulatory integration provoking an equal and opposite pressure for disintegration in terms of strengthening local cultural identities and of regions asserting their right to be heard. The debate on the future shape of higher education is following the same track. The diversity of institutions and even systems of higher education across the European Union should be nurtured against the tide of globalised orthodoxy based on the present league tables. The European higher education classification is a key part of this process for Strathclyde, as for every European university.

References

Clark, B.R. (1998). *Creating Entrepreneurial Universities. Organizational Pathways of Transformation*. Oxford/New York: Pergamon/IAU Press.
Figel, J. (2008). Speech presented at launch of European Commission University/Industry Forum, Brussels, February.
Florian, R.V. (2007). Irreproducibility of the results of the Shanghai academic ranking of world universities. *Scientometrics*, 72(1), 25–32, doi: 10.1007/x11192-007-1712-1.
Hood, J. (2006). Paper presented at annual conference of the Association of Heads of University Administrations, University of Oxford, 4 April.
Higher Education Funding Council for England (HEFCE). (2008). *Counting what is measured, or measuring what counts? League and their impact on higher education institutions in England.* Report to HEFCE by the Center for Higher Education Research and Information (CHERI), Open University & Hobsons Research. HEFCE Issues Paper, 2008/14.
Times Higher Education (THE). (2008). Free sector and let fees rise, argue Lords, 3 July.

Name Index

Subject Index

Printed in the United States
141628LV00006B/32/P